Laws and Legislation Series

FEDERAL TORTS REFORM, CLAIMS AND LIABILITY

LAWS AND LEGISLATION SERIES

State Secrets Protection Act
Lara H. Nellington (Editor)
2009 ISBN: 978-1-60692-711-3

Revisiting and Evaluating the Congressional Review Act
Katherine R. Williamson (Editor)
2009 ISBN: 978-1-60692-687-1

Clean Diamond Trade Act
James T. Williams (Editor)
2009. ISBN: 978-1-60741-111-6

Federal Torts Reform, Claims and Liability
Ben V. Colligan (Editor)
2009. ISBN: 978-1-60692-989-6

Laws and Legislation Series

FEDERAL TORTS REFORM, CLAIMS AND LIABILITY

BEN V. COLLIGAN
EDITOR

Nova Science Publishers, Inc.
New York

For permission to use material from this book please contact us:
Telephone 631-231-7269; Fax 631-231-8175
Web Site: http://www.novapublishers.com

LIBRARY OF CONGRESS CATALOGING-IN-PUBLICATION DATA

Available upon request.
ISBN: 978-1-60692-989-6

Published by Nova Science Publishers, Inc. ✛ New York

CONTENTS

PREFACE

The Federal Tort Claims Act is the statute by which the United States authorizes tort suits to be brought against itself. With exceptions, it makes the United States liable for injuries caused by the negligent or wrongful act or omission of any federal employee acting within the scope of his employment, in accordance with the law of the state where the act or omission occurred. Three major exceptions, under which the United States may not be held liable, even in circumstances where a private person could be held liable under state law, are the Feres doctrine, which prohibits suits by military personnel for injuries sustained incident to service; the discretionary function exception, which immunizes the United States for acts or omissions of its employees that involve policy decisions; and the intentional tort exception, which precludes suits against the United States for assault and battery, among some other intentional torts, unless they are committed by federal law enforcement or investigative officials. This book discusses, among other things, the application of the Feres doctrine to suits for injuries caused by medical malpractice in the military, the prohibition of suits by victims of atomic testing, Supreme Court cases interpreting the discretionary function exception, the extent to which federal employees may be held liable for torts they commit in the scope of their employment, and the government contractor defense to products liability design defect suits.

Chapter 1 - This chapter considers the constitutionality of federal tort reform legislation, such as the products liability and medical malpractice reform proposals that have been introduced for the last several Congresses. Tort law at present is almost exclusively state law rather than federal law, although, as noted in the appendix to this chapter, Congress has enacted a number of tort reform statutes.

Part I of this chapter concludes that Congress has the authority to enact tort reform legislation generally, under its power to regulate interstate commerce, and to make such legislation applicable to intrastate torts, because tort suits generally affect interstate commerce. However, it may be unconstitutional for tort reform legislation to be applied to particular intrastate torts that do not substantially affect interstate commerce.

In concluding that Congress has the authority to enact tort reform "generally," we refer to reforms that have been widely implemented at the state level, such as caps on damages and limitations on joint and several liability and on the collateral source rule. More specialized types of reforms are not necessarily immune from constitutional challenge. For example, some state courts have struck down statutes that provide that a portion of punitive damages awards must be paid to state funds (although other state courts have upheld such statutes).

Part I also concludes that there would appear to be no due process or federalism (or any other constitutional) impediments to Congress's limiting a state common law right of recovery. The only exception concerns requiring alternative dispute resolution that limits the right to a jury trial.

Part II considers alternative dispute resolution alternatives, some of which could have constitutional problems. The Seventh Amendment would preclude Congress from eliminating the right to a jury trial in common law tort actions brought in federal court. Congress may, however, eliminate the right to bring common law tort actions in federal court, or eliminate common law tort actions themselves.

Congress apparently may create Article I tribunals, such as arbitration panels, to hear tort claims, if it alters tort claims so that they are no longer traditional common law actions (but rather are like no-fault workers' compensation claims), or if it allows *de novo* review by an Article III court, with the right to a jury trial, of traditional common law tort actions (rather than allow merely traditional appellate review). It apparently may also opt for a middle ground by altering the common law cause of action somewhat but not wholly, and by pro-viding for something less than *de novo* review by an Article III court, provided that the Article III court is not required to be too deferential to the findings of the Article I tribunal.

Chapter 2 - The Federal Tort Claims Act is the statute by which the United States authorizes tort suits to be brought against itself. With exceptions, it makes the United States liable for injuries caused by the negligent or wrongful act or omission of any federal employee acting within the scope of his employment, in accordance with the law of the state where the act or omission occurred. Three major exceptions, under which the United States may not be held liable, even in circumstances where a private person could be held liable under state law, are the *Feres* doctrine, which prohibits suits by military personnel for injuries sustained incident to service; the discretionary function exception, which immunizes the United States for acts or omissions of its employees that involve policy decisions; and the intentional tort exception, which precludes suits against the United States for assault and battery, among some other intentional torts, unless they are committed by federal law enforcement or investigative officials.

This chapter discusses, among other things, the application of the *Feres* doctrine to suits for injuries caused by medical malpractice in the military, the prohibition of suits by victims of atomic testing, Supreme Court cases interpreting the discretionary function exception, the extent to which federal employees may be held liable for torts they commit in the scope of their employment, and the government contractor defense to products liability design defect suits.

In the 110th Congress, two bills have been introduced that would amend the Federal Tort Claims Act: H.R. 2249, the Federal Tort Claim Reform Act of 2007, and H.R. 6093, the Carmelo Rodriguez Military Medical Accountability Act of 2008.

Chapter 3 - The Federal Tort Claims Act (FTCA), 28 U.S.C. § 1346(b), 267 1-2680, makes the United States liable, in accordance with the law of the state where a tort occurs, for some of the torts of its employees committed within the scope of their employment. It also makes federal employees immune from all lawsuits arising under state law for torts committed within the scope of their employment. (The FTCA does not prevent a federal employee from being sued for violating the Constitution or a federal statute that authorizes suit against an individual.) Sometimes, Congress wishes to immunize a private organization, or its employees or volunteers, from tort liability. One way it may do so is to enact a statute declaring that the organization or its employees or volunteers shall be deemed federal employees for purposes of the FTCA. This chapter discusses the pros and cons of this type of statute, and then provides examples of more than 50 such statutes.

In: Federal Torts Reform, Claims and Liability ISBN 978-1-60692-989-6
Editor: Ben V. Colligan

Chapter 1

FEDERAL TORT REFORM LEGISLATION: CONSTITUTIONALITY AND SUMMARIES OF SELECTED STATUTES[*]

Henry Cohen and Vanessa K. Burrows

SUMMARY

This chapter considers the constitutionality of federal tort reform legislation, such as the products liability and medical malpractice reform proposals that have been introduced for the last several Congresses. Tort law at present is almost exclusively state law rather than federal law, although, as noted in the appendix to this chapter, Congress has enacted a number of tort reform statutes.

Part I of this chapter concludes that Congress has the authority to enact tort reform legislation generally, under its power to regulate interstate commerce, and to make such legislation applicable to intrastate torts, because tort suits generally affect interstate commerce. However, it may be unconstitutional for tort reform legislation to be applied to particular intrastate torts that do not substantially affect interstate commerce.

In concluding that Congress has the authority to enact tort reform "generally," we refer to reforms that have been widely implemented at the state level, such as

---

[*] This is an edited, excerpted and augmented edition of a Congressional Research Service Report for Congress publication, Order Code 95-797, dated September 29, 2008.

caps on damages and limitations on joint and several liability and on the collateral source rule. More specialized types of reforms are not necessarily immune from constitutional challenge. For example, some state courts have struck down statutes that provide that a portion of punitive damages awards must be paid to state funds (although other state courts have upheld such statutes).

Part I also concludes that there would appear to be no due process or federalism (or any other constitutional) impediments to Congress's limiting a state common law right of recovery. The only exception concerns requiring alternative dispute resolution that limits the right to a jury trial.

Part II considers alternative dispute resolution alternatives, some of which could have constitutional problems. The Seventh Amendment would preclude Congress from eliminating the right to a jury trial in common law tort actions brought in federal court. Congress may, however, eliminate the right to bring common law tort actions in federal court, or eliminate common law tort actions themselves.

Congress apparently may create Article I tribunals, such as arbitration panels, to hear tort claims, if it alters tort claims so that they are no longer traditional common law actions (but rather are like no-fault workers' compensation claims), or if it allows *de novo* review by an Article III court, with the right to a jury trial, of traditional common law tort actions (rather than allow merely traditional appellate review). It apparently may also opt for a middle ground by altering the common law cause of action somewhat but not wholly, and by pro-viding for something less than *de novo* review by an Article III court, provided that the Article III court is not required to be too deferential to the findings of the Article I tribunal.

PART I. TORT REFORM GENERALLY

Introduction

This chapter considers the constitutionality of federal tort reform legislation, such as the products liability and medical malpractice reform proposals that have been introduced for the last several Congresses. A tort is a civil (as opposed to a criminal) wrong, other than a breach of contract, that causes injury for which the victim may sue to recover damages. Torts include negligent acts, such as medical malpractice, and acts, such as selling defective products, for which one can be held strictly liable (liable even in the absence of negligence). Tort law at present is almost exclusively state law rather than federal law, although, as noted in the appendix to this chapter, Congress has enacted a number of tort reform statutes.

Part I of this chapter concludes that enactment of tort reform legislation generally would appear to be within Congress's power to regulate commerce, and would not appear to violate principles of due process or federalism. However, it may be unconstitutional for tort reform legislation to be applied to particular intrastate torts that do not substantially affect interstate commerce. In concluding that Congress has the authority to enact tort reform "generally," we refer to reforms that have been widely implemented at the state level, such as caps on damages and limitations on joint and several liability and on the collateral source rule. More specialized types of reforms are not necessarily immune from constitutional challenge. For example, some state courts have struck down statutes that provide that a portion of punitive damages awards must be paid to state funds (although other state courts have upheld such statutes).

Part II of this chapter considers alternative dispute resolution alternatives, some of which could have constitutional problems. Part III is a conclusion. The chapter ends with an appendix describing selected federal tort reform statutes.

A. Commerce Power

A federal statute is constitutional if it is enacted pursuant to a power of Congress enumerated in the Constitution and if it does not contravene any provision of the Constitution. The enumerated power pursuant to which federal tort reform could be enacted is Congress's power "To regulate Commerce with foreign Nations, and among the several States" (Art. I, § 8, cl. 3).[1] One might ask, however, whether tort law is "commerce," and, if it is, whether federal tort reform legislation would be constitutional as applied to purely *intrastate* torts.

The Supreme Court has held that Congress's power to regulate interstate commerce includes the power to regulate any activity that "exerts a substantial effect on interstate commerce" (*Wicka rd v. Filburn*, 317 U.S. 111, 125 (1942)), or is within a "*class of activities* within the reach of federal power" (*Perez v. United States*, 402 U.S. 146, 154 (1971) (emphasis in original)). Furthermore, "when Congress has determined that an activity affects interstate commerce, the courts need inquire only whether the finding is rational." *Hodel v. Virginia Surface Mining & Reclamation Association, Inc.*, 452 U.S. 264, 277 (1981).[2]

The Supreme Court has held that the business of insurance constitutes interstate commerce for purposes of the Commerce Clause (*United States v. South-Eastern Underwriters Association*, 322 U.S. 533 (1944)), and, whether or not tort reform would in fact substantially affect the business of insurance, it would not appear irrational for Congress to conclude that it would. Consequently, there seems little doubt that tort reform legislation, in general, would be within Congress's commerce power.

However, it may be unconstitutional for tort reform legislation to be applied to particular intrastate torts that arguably do not substantially affect interstate commerce. An example might be an assault by one individual upon another where the assault has no connection with organized crime or any commercial activity. This is because, in *United States v. Lopez*, 514 U.S. 549 (1995), the Supreme Court, for the first time since 1936, declared a federal statute unconstitutional for exceeding Congress's Commerce Clause authority. In *Lopez*, it struck down the Gun-Free School Zones Act of 1990, which made it a federal offense "for any individual knowingly to possess a firearm at a place that the individual knows, or has reasonable cause to believe, is a school zone."

The Court in *Lopez* "identified three broad categories of activity that Congress may regulate under its commerce power. First, Congress may regulate the use of the channels of interstate commerce.[3] Second, Congress is empowered to regulate and protect the instrumentalities of interstate commerce, or things in interstate commerce, even though the threat may come only from intrastate activities. Finally, Congress's commerce authority includes the power to regulate those activities having a substantial relation to interstate commerce, *i.e.*, those activities that substantially affect interstate commerce." *Id.* at 55 8-559 (citations omitted).

The Court in *Lopez* then noted that, if the Gun-Free School Zones Act of 1990 was "to be sustained, it must be under the third category as a regulation of an activity that substantially affects interstate commerce." *Id.* at 559. The act, however, had "nothing to do with 'commerce' or any sort of economic enterprise [and] is not an essential part of a larger regulation of economic activity, in which the regulatory scheme could be undercut unless the intrastate activity were regulated." *Id.* at 561. The same apparently could be said of some torts, such as the assault example suggested above. But it does not appear that it could be said with respect to torts that substantially affect commerce, such as the manufacture of defective products or medical malpractice.

Since *Lopez*, the Supreme Court has decided two major cases on the reach of the Commerce Clause. In *United States v. Morrison*, 529 U.S. 598 (2000), the Court struck down a section of the Violence Against Women Act of 1994 that created a federal cause of action against any person "who commits a crime of violence motivated by gender," whether interstate or intrastate. In striking down the provision, the Court noted that "a fair reading of *Lopez* shows that the noneconomic, criminal nature of the conduct at issue was central to our decision in that case" (*id.* at 610), and "[g]ender-motivated crimes of violence are not, in any sense of the phrase, economic activity."[4] *Id.* at 613.

In *Lopez*, the Court noted that "Congress normally is not required to make formal findings as to the substantial burdens that an activity has on interstate commerce." 514 U.S. at 562. It added, however:

> But to the extent that congressional findings would enable us to evaluate the legislative judgment that the activity in question substantially affected interstate commerce, even though no substantial effect was visible to the naked eye, they are lacking here.

Id. at 563. In *Morrison*, the Court found Congress's findings "substantially weakened" by their reliance on a "but-for causal chain from the initial occurrence of violent crime to every attenuated effect upon interstate commerce." 529 U.S. at 615.

The second recent major Supreme Court case on the reach of the Commerce Clause was *Gonzales v. Raich*, 545 U.S. 1 (2005), which upheld the application of the federal statute prohibiting the manufacture and possession of marijuana to the intrastate cultivation and use of marijuana for medicinal purposes. The Court found that there was a rational basis for concluding that the local cultivation and use of marijuana, "taken in the aggregate, substantially affect[s] interstate commerce." *Id.* at 22. The Court distinguished *Lopez* and *Morrison* on the ground that those two cases involved attempts to regulate activities that were not economic, whereas marijuana is a commodity "for which there is an established, and lucrative, interstate market," and "[p]rohibiting the intrastate possession or manufacture of an article of commerce is a rational (and commonly utilized) means of regulating commerce in that product." *Id.* at 26. *Gonzales v. Raich* appears to support Congress' power to regulate medical malpractice and products liability litigation, because the practice of medicine and the manufacture of products are activities that constitute interstate commerce, and it would be rational to conclude that litigation concerning these activities substantially affects interstate commerce.

B. Due Process

At one time, it might plausibly have been suggested that limitations on tort liability might violate the Fifth Amendment's protection against federal deprivations of property without due process of law. However, in 1978, the Supreme Court, upholding the Price-Anderson Act's limitation on liability for accidents resulting from the operation of privately owned nuclear power plants, wrote:

> Our cases have clearly established that "[a] person has no property, no vested interest, in any rule of common law." The "Constitution does not forbid the creation of new rights, or the abolition of old ones recognized by the common law, to attain a permissible legislative object," despite the fact that "otherwise settled expectations" may be upset thereby. Indeed, statutes limiting liability are relatively commonplace and have consistently been enforced by the courts.

Duke Power Co. v. Carolina Environmental Study Group, 438 U.S. 59, 88, n.32 (1978) (citations omitted).

In 1985, the Supreme Court, without written opinions, upheld the constitutionality of California statutes that placed caps in medical malpractice cases on, respectively, noneconomic damages and lawyers' contingent fees.[5]

C. Federalism

In *National League of Cities v. Usery*, 426 U.S. 833, 855 (1976), the Supreme Court held that the Fair Labor Standards Act, 29 U.S.C. §§ 201 *et seq.*, which prescribes the federal minimum wage, could not constitutionally be applied to employees of state and municipal governments. There was no contention that Congress' commerce power was not broad enough to encompass this sort of regulation. The contention, rather, which the Court accepted, was that the Constitution contained an affirmative limitation on this exercise of the commerce power. The Court did not name any particular provision of the Constitution as imposing the limitation in this case, but did quote an earlier case that said that the Tenth Amendment "expressly declares the constitutional policy that Congress may not exercise power in a fashion that impairs the States' integrity or their ability to function effectively in a federal system."[6]

In any event, the Court held that the Commerce Clause did not authorize Congress "to directly displace the States' freedom to structure integral operations in areas of traditional governmental functions." *Id.* at 852. The only example the Court gave of an integral governmental function was the structuring of "employer-employee relationships in such areas as fire prevention, police protection, sanitation, public health, and parks and recreation." *Id.* at 851. It added, however, that "[t]hese examples are obviously not an exhaustive catalogue." *Id.* at 851 n.16.

In *Garcia v. San Antonio Metropolitan Transit Authority*, 469 U.S. 528 (1985), the Court overruled *National League of Cities*, holding that the Fair Labor Standards Act could be applied to state and municipal employees. It concluded that the *National League of Cities* test for "integral operations in areas of traditional governmental functions" had proven both "impractical and doctrinally barren," and that the Court in 1976 had "tried to repair what did not need repair." *Id.* at 557. The Court found that it had "no license to employ freestanding conceptions of state sovereignty when measuring congressional authority under the Commerce Clause." *Id.* at 550. The Court did, however, "recognize that the States occupy a special and specific position in our constitutional system and that the scope of Congress' authority under the Commerce Clause must reflect that position." *Id.* at 556.

Subsequently, the Court took a step back in the direction of *National League of Cities*. In *New York v. United States*, 505 U.S. 144 (1992), the Court invalidated a provision of the Low-Level Radioactive Waste Policy Amendments Act of 1985 because it required states not participating in a regional waste disposal compact to "take title" to waste or accept liability for generators' damages. The Court readily acknowledged that Congress may regulate the interstate market in disposal of low- level radioactive waste, but noted that the Commerce Clause "authorizes Congress to regulate interstate commerce directly; it does not authorize Congress to regulate state governments' regulation of interstate commerce." *Id.* at 166.

The Court discussed two methods "by which Congress may urge a State to adopt a legislative program consistent with federal interests. First, under Congress' spending power, 'Congress may attach conditions on the receipt of federal funds.' Second, where Congress has the authority to regulate private activity under the Commerce Clause, we have recognized Congress' power to offer States the choice of regulating that activity according to federal standards or having state law preempted by federal regulation." *Id.* at 167.

But if states decline to participate in a federal scheme, Congress may not force them to do so; to have its way, Congress must preempt state law and regulate directly. The "take title" provision, rather than presenting states with a choice between regulatory participation or accepting federal preemption, required states to choose "between two unconstitutionally coercive regulatory techniques Either way, 'the Act commandeers the legislative processes of the States by directly compelling them to enact and enforce a federal regulatory program.'" *Id.* at 176.[7]

Under *New York v. United States*, the only significant federalism restraint on exercise of the commerce power is that state regulatory processes may not be "commandeered" for federal purposes; there is no federalism restraint on federal regulation of businesses and individuals in areas traditionally regulated by states. The fact that Congress has traditionally deferred in large measure to state regulation of the insurance industry, for example, does not mean that Congress must continue to do so; Congress does not invade areas reserved to the states by the Tenth Amendment "simply because it exercises its authority in a manner that displaces the States' exercise of their police powers." *Hodel v. Virginia Surface Mining & Reclamation Association, Inc.*, 452 U.S. 264, 291 (1981) (upholding "steep slope" and other federal regulations of surface mining in spite of traditional state role in regulating land use).

In the case of federal tort reform proposals such as reducing awards by amounts recovered from collateral sources, Congress would not be commandeering state regulatory processes. Congress would merely be enacting federal law that preempted substantive state law, and requiring states to enforce the federal law. In *New York v. United States*, the Court cited four cases that discuss "the well established power of Congress to pass laws enforceable in state courts." *Id.* at 178. The Court added:

> These cases involve no more than an application of the Supremacy Clause's provision that federal law "shall be the supreme Law of the Land," enforceable in every State. More to the point, all involve congressional regulation of individuals, not congressional requirements that States regulate. Federal statutes enforceable in state courts do, in a sense, direct state judges to enforce them, but this sort of federal "direction" of state judges is mandated by the text of the Supremacy Clause.

Id. at 178-179. One of the four cases the Supreme Court cited, *Second Employers' Liability Cases*, 223 U.S. 1 (1912), involved what today would be called tort reform. The case was a challenge to the Employers' Liability Act of 1908, which regulated the liability of common carriers by railroad to their employees; it was essentially a federal workers' compensation statute that preempted state tort law by, among other things, its "abrogation of the fellow-servant rule, the extension of the carrier's liability to cases of death, and the restriction of the defenses of contributory negligence and assumption of risk " *Id.*

at 49. One question before the Supreme Court was "whether rights arising under the congressional act may be enforced, as of right, in the courts of the States when their jurisdiction, as prescribed by local laws, is adequate to the occasion." *Id.* at 55. The Court answered the question as follows:

> When Congress, in the exertion of the power confided to it by the Constitution, adopted that act, it spoke for all the people and all the States, and thereby established policy for all. That policy is as much the policy of Connecticut as it the act had emanated from its own legislature, and should be respected accordingly in the courts of the State. *Id.* at 57.

Part II. Alternative Dispute Resolution

One tort reform that may be considered by Congress is to require that tort claims — particularly medical malpractice claims — be decided by alternative dispute resolution (ADR) procedures, such as binding arbitration, rather than by traditional jury trials. When Congress creates a federal cause of action, it is generally free to prescribe any procedure for its enforcement, with or without a jury trial.[8] Traditional tort actions, however, such as medical malpractice and products liability, are not federal causes of action; they are governed by state law, even when they are brought in federal court on diversity grounds.[9] State laws generally provide for jury trials in tort cases brought in state courts,[10] and the Seventh Amendment to the United States Constitution generally provides for jury trials of cases arising under state law that are brought in federal court.[11] The question has arisen, therefore, as to the extent to which the Constitution permits Congress to require alternative dispute resolution, in federal or state forums, of tort claims arising under state law.

A. Seventh Amendment

If Congress were to require ADR procedures in lieu of jury trials, then the Seventh Amendment would become a consideration. The Seventh Amendment guarantees the right to trial by jury "In Suits at common law, where the value in controversy shall exceed twenty dollars."[12] Tort actions are suits at common law, so the Seventh Amendment applies to them.[13] However, the Seventh Amendment, unlike most of the Bill of Rights, does not apply in state courts,[14] where most tort actions are brought. It does apply, however, to cases arising under state law that are brought in federal court on diversity grounds.[15]

Therefore, Congress may not eliminate the right to a jury trial in common law tort actions brought in federal court. It may, however, eliminate the right to bring common law tort actions in federal court. One way to do this would be to abolish diversity jurisdiction in tort suits; i.e., to prohibit tort suits arising under state law from being brought in federal courts.[16] Another way would be to alter tort suits to the point that they could no longer be considered "Suits at common law" to which the Seventh Amendment would apply.

Congress has done the latter with respect to torts inflicted upon federal workers in the workplace. The Federal Employees' Compensation Act, 5 U.S.C. §§ 8101 *et seq.*, provides for compensation to federal employees for disability or death resulting from work-related injuries, whether the result of a tort or otherwise. Employees can recover without proof of fault on the part of the government or its employees, but are prohibited from bringing a tort action arising under state law against the government or its employees.[17] An injured employee seeking recovery must file a claim with the Secretary of Labor, who determines whether the employee is entitled to an award. There is no right to a jury trial, nor to judicial review. The Supreme Court has held that such an arrangement does not violate the Seventh Amendment because it "abolishes all right of recovery in ordinary cases, and therefore leaves nothing to be tried by jury."[18]

It appears, therefore, that Congress may prohibit common law tort suits from being brought in federal court, but may not take the less radical step of allowing them to be brought in federal court but prohibiting them from being heard by juries. If Congress may not require common law tort suits to be heard by a federal court without a jury, then it also may not require them to be decided by a federally established arbitration panel or other federally established non-judicial forum.[19] To do so would violate not only the Seventh Amendment; it would violate Article III of the Constitution.

B. Article III

Article III, section 1, provides that the judicial power of the United States shall be vested in one supreme court, and in such inferior courts as Congress may establish, and that the judges of both the supreme and inferior courts shall hold life tenure "during good Behavior," at an irreducible compensation. Federal courts created under this provision are commonly known as "Article III courts." In addition, however, Congress, pursuant to its powers enumerated in Article I, may establish Article I "legislative" courts in "specialized areas having particularized needs and warranting distinctive treatment."[20] Article I judges need not be granted life tenure or irreducible salaries.

However, since only Article III courts may exercise the judicial power of the United States, Congress' power to create Article I courts is limited to the above "specialized areas." Except in these areas, Congress may not provide for federal judicial power to be exercised by federally established arbitration panels, or by any federal forum other than an Article III court.

In *Northern Pipeline Construction Co. v. Marathon Pipeline Co.*, the Supreme Court "identified three situations in which Art. III does not bar the creation of legislative courts."[21] These three situations are territorial courts, military courts, and courts created to adjudicate cases involving "public rights."[22] With respect to the third situation, *Marathon* elaborated:

> [A] matter of public rights must at a minimum arise "between the government and others." In contrast, "the liability of one individual to another under the law as defined," is a matter of private rights. Our precedents clearly establish that *only* controversies in the former category may be removed from Art. III courts and delegated to legislative courts or administrative agencies for their determination. Private-rights disputes, on the other hand, lie at the core of the historically recognized judicial power.[23]

Subsequently, the Court rejected the notion that public rights must at a minimum arise between the government and others.[24] In *Granfinanciera, S.A. v. No rdberg*, the Court wrote:

> The crucial question, in cases not involving the Federal Government, is whether "Congress, acting for a valid legislative purpose pursuant to its constitutional powers under Article I, [has] create[d] a seemingly 'private' right that is so closely integrated into a public regulatory scheme as to be a matter appropriate for agency resolution with limited involvement by the Article III judiciary." If a statutory right is not closely intertwined with a federal regulatory program Congress has power to enact, and if that right neither belongs to nor exists against the Federal Government, then it must be adjudicated by an Article III court.[25]

C. Article III / Seventh Amendment Equivalence

The constitutional problem with placing common law tort actions in an Article I tribunal is equivalent to the constitutional problem with denying jury trials in such cases. In *Granfinanciera, S.A. v. Nordberg*, the Court noted that Congress cannot

> conjure away the Seventh Amendment by mandating that traditional legal [*i.e.*, common law] claims be taken to an administrative tribunal. In certain situations, of course, Congress may fashion causes of action that are closely *analogous* to common-law claims and place them beyond the ambit of the Seventh Amendment by assigning their resolution to a forum in which jury trials are unavailable. Congress' power to do so is limited, however, just as its power to place adjudicative authority in non-Article III tribunals is circumscribed.[26]

That is, the situations in which Congress may deny the right to a jury trial are the same situations in which Congress may place a matter outside of an Article III court. In the Court's words:

> [I]f a statutory cause of action is legal [*i.e.*, common law] in nature, the question whether the Seventh Amendment permits Congress to assign its adjudication to a tribunal that does not employ juries as factfinders requires the same answer as the question whether Article III allows Congress to assign adjudication of that cause of action to a non-Article III tribunal. [I]f the action must be tried under the auspices of an Article III court, then the Seventh Amendment affords the parties a right to a jury trial whenever the cause of action is legal [*i.e.*, common law] in nature. Conversely, if Congress may assign the adjudication of a statutory cause of action to a non-Article III tribunal, then the Seventh Amendment poses no independent bar to the adjudication of that action by a nonjury factfinder.[27]

D. Applying Article III and the Seventh Amendment

Whether a federal statute requiring tort claims to be decided by an Article I tribunal would violate Article III, and whether it would violate the Seventh Amendment, amount to the same question. But what is the answer? Before examining some Supreme Court decisions that may shed light on it, we should emphasize that the question arises only if Congress were to establish a federal non- Article III forum to hear traditional tort claims. If Congress instead were simply to prohibit states from using jury trials in tort cases, but did not establish an Article I forum for such cases, then it might raise another constitutional issue (which is discussed in Section F, below) but it would not raise an Article III / Seventh Amendment issue.[28] This is because state courts were created pursuant to state laws or constitutions and do not exercise federal judicial power, and because the Seventh Amendment does not apply to them.

But to what extent may Congress require that tort claims be decided by an Article I tribunal? In *Thomas v. Union Carbide Agricultural Products Co.*, the Supreme Court noted that *Northern Pipeline* had established "that Congress may not vest in a non-Article III court the power to adjudicate, render final judgment, and issue binding orders in a traditional contract action arising under state law, without consent of the litigants, and subject only to ordinary appellate review."[29] The same undoubtedly applies to traditional tort actions arising under state law. However, this quotation suggests that Congress may vest tort claims in a non-Article III forum if it does at least one of two things: (1) alters tort claims so that they are no longer traditional common law actions, or (2) allows *de novo* review, with the right to a jury trial, of traditional common law tort actions, rather than allow merely traditional appellate review. In other words, Congress apparently may require that traditional common law tort actions initially be heard in a federal non-Article III forum, without a jury, provided it allows a dissatisfied party to then seek a jury trial.[30] However, if Congress wishes to limit judicial review of tort claims, then it apparently must alter tort claims so that they are no longer traditional common law tort actions.

To what extent must Congress alter tort claims in order to place them in a non- Article III forum and not provide *de novo* review? In *Granfinanciera*, the Court held that "Congress may fashion causes of action that are closely *analogous* to common- law claims and place them beyond the gambit of the Seventh Amendment" if, in cases not involving the federal government, the private right that Congress creates "is so closely integrated into a public regulatory scheme as to be a matter appropriate for agency resolution with limited involvement by the Article III judiciary."[31] In *Thomas*, the Court indicated that such limited involvement may consist in judicial review that is something less than *de novo* review with the right to a jury trial.

In *Thomas*, the Court rejected the notion that a matter of public rights must at a minimum arise between the government and others.[32] Instead, it held "that practical attention to substance rather than doctrinaire reliance on formal categories should inform application of Article III."[33] *Thomas* involved a provision of the Federal Insecticide, Fungicide, and Rodenticide Act (FIFRA), 7 U.S C. § § 136 *et seq.* FIFRA requires manufacturers, as a precondition for registration of a pesticide, to submit research data to the Environmental Protection Agency (EPA) concerning the product's health, safety, and environmental effects. Congress wished to allow the EPA to consider data submitted by one registrant to support the registration of the same or a similar product by another registrant, and therefore "provided statutory authority for the use of previously submitted data as well as a scheme for sharing the costs of data generation."[34] In order to avoid a "logjam of litigation that resulted from controversies over data compensation," Congress provided for "a system of negotiation and binding arbitration to resolve compensation disputes among registrants."[35] "The arbitrator's decision is subject to judicial review only for 'fraud, misrepresentation, or other misconduct.'"[36]

The Court considered several factors in determining that an Article III tribunal was not required to resolve these disputes. It found mandatory binding arbitration permissible in part because the right to compensation for shared data "does not depend on or replace a right to compensation under state law."[37]

> The right created by FIFRA is not purely a "private" right, but bears many of the characteristics of a "public" right. Use of a registrant's data to support a follow- on [*i.e.*, subsequent] registration serves a public purpose as an integral part of a program safeguarding the public health. Congress has the power, under Article I, to authorize an agency administering a complex regulatory scheme to allocate costs and benefits among voluntary participants in the program without providing an Article III adjudication.[38]

Thus, to use the words of the Court in *Granfinanciera* a few years later, *Thomas* involved a private right that was "closely integrated into a public regulatory scheme."[39] In addition, the Court in *Thomas* cited the fact that "no unwilling defendant is subjected to judicial enforcement power as a result of the agency 'adjudication,'"[40] and that FIFRA, while it limits judicial review, it "does not preclude review of the arbitration proceeding by an Article III court."[41]

In *Commodity Futures Trading Commission v. Schor*, the Supreme Court again emphasized that, in determining whether an Article III tribunal is required, it

> has declined to adopt formalistic and unbending rules. Although such rules might lend a greater degree of coherence to this area of law, they might also unduly restrict Congress' ability to take needed and innovative action pursuant to its Article I powers. Thus, in reviewing Article III challenges, we have weighed a number of factors, none of which has been deemed determinative, with an eye to the practical effect that the congressional action will have on the constitutionally assigned role of the federal judiciary.[42]

The opinion in *Schor* reveals how nonformalistic the Court's approach is in this area:

> Among the factors upon which we have focused are the extent to which the "essential attributes of judicial power" are reserved to Article III courts, and, conversely, the extent to which the non-Article III forum exercises the range of jurisdiction and powers normally vested only in Article III courts, the origins and importance of the right to be adjudicated, and the concerns that drove Congress to depart from the requirements of Article III.[43]

The Court in *Schor* upheld a congressional grant of adjudicatory powers to a federal agency, the Commodity Futures Trading Commission (CFTC). The Court emphasized that the CFTC's

> adjudicatory powers depart from the traditional agency model in just one respect: the CFTC's jurisdiction over common law counterclaims. Aside from its authorization of counterclaim jurisdiction, the [statute] leaves far more of the "essential attributes of judicial power" to Article III courts than did that portion of the Bankruptcy Act found unconstitutional in *Northern Pipeline*.[44]

Specifically, CFTC orders are reviewed under the "weight of the evidence" standard, "rather than the more deferential standard found lacking in *Northern Pipeline*." Furthermore, "[t]he legal rulings of the CFTC are subject to *de novo* review."[45]

In *Northern Pipeline* the Court found unconstitutional the delegation to an Article I tribunal — the United States Bankruptcy Court — of the adjudication of the right to recover contract damages. Although discharge in bankruptcy "may well be a 'public right'" and if it is may be delegated to an Article I court, the right to recover contract damages is a state-created private right and as such may not be delegated to an Article I court.[46] In response to the argument that "the bankruptcy court is merely an 'adjunct' to the district court, and that the delegation of certain adjudicative functions to the bankruptcy court is accordingly consistent with the principle that the judicial power of the United States must be vested in Art. III courts,"[47] the Supreme Court observed that "the judgments of the bankruptcy courts are apparently subject to review only under the more deferential 'clearly erroneous' standard."[48] Such limited review gave the bankruptcy courts more power than was permissible for an "adjunct."

In *Granfinanciera*, the Court held that the Seventh Amendment requires a jury trial in a suit by a trustee in bankruptcy to recover an allegedly fraudulent monetary transfer. It reached this conclusion because

> a bankruptcy trustee's right to recover a fraudulent conveyance under 11 U.S.C. § 548(a)(2) seems to us more accurately characterized as a private right rather than a public right as we have used those terms in our Article III decisions. In *Northern Pipeline Construction Co.* the plurality noted that state-law causes of action for breach of contract or warranty are paradigmatic private rights, even when asserted by an insolvent corporation in the midst of Chapter 11 reorganization proceedings.[49]

It was not sufficient that Congress had "reclassified a pre-existing, common-law cause of action. Congress cannot eliminate a party's Seventh Amendment right to a jury trial merely by relabeling the cause of action to which it attaches and placing exclusive jurisdiction in an administrative agency or a specialized court of equity."[50]

"Nor," the Court added, "can Congress' assignment be justified on the ground that jury trials of fraudulent conveyance actions would 'go far to dismantle the statutory scheme,' or that bankruptcy proceedings have been placed in 'an administrative forum with which the jury would be incompatible.'"[51]

Furthermore, "[i]t may be that providing jury trials in some fraudulent conveyance actions would impede swift resolution of bankruptcy proceedings and increase the expense of Chapter 11 reorganizations. But 'these considerations are insufficient to overcome the clear command of the Seventh Amendment.'"[52]

E. Constitutionality of Establishing Federal Non-Article III Forums: Conclusion

In *Thomas*, the Court upheld the use of a non-Article III forum because, among other things, the right created was "not purely a 'private' right," and limited judicial review by an Article III court was permitted.[53] In *Schor*, the Court upheld the use of a non-Article III forum because, among other things, its adjudicatory powers over common law actions were limited, its orders were reviewed by an Article III court under a relatively non-deferential standard, and its legal rulings were subject to *de novo* review.

In *Northern Pipeline*, the Court struck down the use of an Article I forum because it was allowed to decide state-created private rights, and its decisions were subject only to deferential judicial review. In *Granfinanciera*, the Court struck down the use of an Article I forum because the right that was adjudicated was a private right.

These cases show that, as the Court wrote in *Schor*, "in reviewing Article III challenges, we have weighed a number of factors, none of which has been deemed determinative, with an eye to the practical effect that the congressional action will have on the constitutionally assigned role of the federal judiciary."[54] However, the major factors appear to be the extent to which the cause of action constitutes a private right, and the degree of review by an Article III tribunal that is provided. If a cause of action is a traditional common law cause of action, not closely integrated into a federal regulatory scheme, then *de novo* review by an Article III court, with a jury trial, would apparently be required. If the cause of action is altered somewhat, but still resembles a common law action, then something less than *de novo* review by an Article III court might be adequate, provided the Article III court is not required to be too deferential to the finding of the non-Article III forum. If the cause of action is altered to the point that it no longer resembles a common law tort, and is closely integrated into a federal regulatory scheme, then adjudication by an Article I forum, without judicial review, may be permissible. It does not seem possible to be more specific than this, as "bright-line rules cannot effectively be employed to yield broad principles applicable to all Article III inquiries."[55]

F. Constitutionality of Prohibiting States from Using Jury Trials, without Establishment of a Federal Non-Article III Forum

As noted above, if Congress were to prohibit the states from using jury trials in tort cases, but did not establish a federal non-Article III forum to hear such cases, then it would raise no Article III / Seventh Amendment issue, but it would raise another constitutional issue. This issue is whether Congress, even where it would otherwise have the power to regulate under the Commerce Clause, may alter the procedures that state courts use to adjudicate state causes of action. In *New York v. United States*, discussed at page 5, above, the Court prohibited Congress from using its commerce power to commandeer state regulatory processes. Although, as noted, this restriction would not seem to preclude Congress from preempting substantive state law, it might be argued that eliminating jury trials, constituting as it would an interference with state court procedure, might amount to commandeering state regulatory processes.

This distinction between substance and procedure also finds support in the Supreme Court's approach to diversity cases, which are cases arising under state law which, because they are between citizens of different states and the amount in controversy exceeds $50,000, may be heard in federal court. 28 U.S.C. § 1332. In

Erie Railroad Co. v. Tompkins, 304 U.S. 64, 78 (1937), the Supreme Court held that, in diversity cases, a federal court is bound by the substantive, as opposed to the procedural, law of the state in which it sits, "whether the law of the State shall be declared by its Legislature in a statute or by its highest court in a decision."[56]

In *Guaranty Trust Co. v. New York*, 326 U.S. 99 (1945), the Supreme Court held that statutes of limitations are substantive for this purpose, and that therefore federal courts must apply state statutes of limitations in diversity cases. By "substantive," the Court meant that the statute could substantially affect the outcome of the litigation. A statute of limitations can substantially affect the outcome of litigation because it can preclude an action from even being brought. By contrast, the right to a jury trial does not have a comparably substantial effect, because in a non-jury trial a judge presumably applies the same law to the same facts as a jury would in a jury trial.

In diversity cases, "[i]t is now clear that federal law determines whether there is a right to a jury trial in a case in federal court and that state law is wholly irrelevant."[57] Although the Seventh Amendment, rather than the substantive/procedural distinction, is the main factor here, one could nevertheless argue that, if federal courts may use the federal rule with respect to jury trials of state causes of action, then state courts may not be preempted from using their own rules with respect to jury trials of state causes of action.

In addition, "[t]he general rule, bottomed deeply in belief in the importance of state control of state judicial procedure, is that federal law takes the state courts as it finds them. For example, state rules about the ways in which claims for relief, or defenses, or counter-defenses, must be asserted may ordinarily be applied also to federal claims and defenses and counter-defenses, providing only that the rules are not so rigorous as, in effect, to nullify the asserted rights."[58]

This general rule seems to have operated in a 1950 case in which the Supreme Court held that a state may "deny access to its courts to persons seeking recovery under the Federal Employers' Liability Act if in similar cases the State for reasons of local policy denies resort to its courts and enforces its policy impartially so as not to involve a discrimination against Employers' Liability Act suits ."[59]

There is an apparently strong argument, however, in support of Congress' power to eliminate jury trials in state causes of action heard in state courts. The Supreme Court has held that section 2 of the Federal Arbitration Act, 9 U.S.C. § 2, preempts conflicting state law. This statute provides that agreements to arbitrate "shall be valid, irrevocable, and enforceable," and thus effectively eliminates the right to a jury trial in some state cases. In *Southland Corp. v. Keating*, 465 U.S. 1, 11 (1984), the Supreme Court found that "[t]he Federal Arbitration Act rests on the authority of Congress to enact substantive rules under the Commerce Clause," and that it preempted a state statute that had been interpreted to require judicial consideration of claims brought under a state statute. In *Perry v. Thomas*, 482 U.S. 483 (1987), and in *Doctor's Associates, Inc. v. Casarotto*, 517 U.S. 681 (1996), the Supreme Court again found the Federal Arbitration Act to preempt conflicting state law. If Congress can eliminate judicial consideration of a case, then arguably it can eliminate jury consideration while retaining judicial consideration.

Part III. Conclusion

A. Tort Reform Generally

Congress has the authority to enact tort reform legislation generally, under its power to regulate interstate commerce, and to make such legislation applicable to intrastate torts, because tort suits generally affect interstate commerce. However, it may be unconstitutional for tort reform legislation to be applied to particular intrastate torts that arguably do not substantially affect interstate commerce.

There would appear to be no due process or federalism (or any other constitutional) impediments to Congress' limiting a state common law right of recovery. The only exception concerns requiring alternative dispute resolution that limits the right to a jury trial.

Alternative Dispute Resolution

The Seventh Amendment would preclude Congress from eliminating the right to a jury trial in common law tort actions brought in federal court. Congress may, however, eliminate the right to bring common law tort actions in federal court, or eliminate common law tort actions themselves.

Congress apparently may create Article I tribunals, such as arbitration panel, to hear tort claims, if it alters tort claims so that they are no longer traditional common law actions (but rather are like no-fault workers' compensation claims), or if it allows *de novo* review by an Article III court, with the right to a jury trial, of traditional common law tort actions (rather than allow merely traditional appellate review). It apparently may also opt for a middle ground by altering the common law cause of action somewhat but not wholly, and by providing for something less than *de novo* review by an Article III court, provided that the

Article III court is not required to be too deferential to the findings of the Article I tribunal.

Finally, a strong argument may be made that Congress has the power to eliminate jury trials in tort actions brought in state court, but this is uncertain.

APPENDIX. SELECTED FEDERAL TORT REFORM STATUTES

Employers Liability Act of 1908, 35 Stat. 65, c. 149

This statute regulated the liability of common carriers by railroad to their employees; it was essentially a federal workers' compensation statute that preempted state tort law by, among other things, its "abrogation of the fellow-servant rule, the extension of the carrier's liability to cases of death, and the restriction of the defenses of contributory negligence and assumption of risk " *Mondou v. New York, N.H. & H.R. Co.*, 223 U.S. 1, 49 (1912). In this case, the Supreme Court upheld the constitutionality of the statute, including the power of Congress to regulate commerce to override state tort law. The Court wrote:

> When Congress, in the exertion of the power confided to it by the Constitution, adopted that act, it spoke for all the people and all the States, and thereby established policy for all. That policy is as much the policy of Connecticut as it the act had emanated from its own legislature, and should be respected accordingly in the courts of the State. *Id.* at 57.

Price-Anderson Act, 42 U.S.C. § 221 0(e)

This statute limits the tort liability of Nuclear Regulatory Commission licensees (such as nuclear power plants) and Department of Energy nuclear contractors for a single "nuclear incident." For example, for nuclear power plants, the liability limit is pegged to the amount of financial protection required of the licensee under a two- tiered system of privately available insurance plus industrywide pro-rata contributions. That total, including a 5 percent "surcharge" provided for in the act, is currently $9.09 billion.

In *Duke Power Co. v. Carolina Environmental Study Group*, 438 U.S. 59, 88, n.32 (1978), the Supreme Court upheld the constitutionality of the act, writing:

> Our cases have clearly established that "[a] person has no property, no vested interest, in any rule of common law." The "Constitution does not forbid the creation of new rights, or the abolition of old ones recognized by the common law, to attain a permissible legislative object," despite the fact that "otherwise settled expectations" may be upset thereby. Indeed, statutes limiting liability are relatively commonplace and have consistently been enforced by the courts [citations omitted].

Atomic Testing Liability Act, 42 U.S.C. § 2212

This 1990 statute, which reenacted the Warner Amendment, § 1631 of P.L. 98- 525 (1984), made the Federal Tort Claims Act the exclusive remedy for suits against government contractors who carried out atomic weapons testing programs that caused injury or death due to exposure to radiation. In other words, this law immunized the contractors from liability under state tort law and made the United States liable in their place.[60] Two federal courts of appeals upheld the constitutionality of the Warner Amendment.[61]

Other Statutes that Substitute the United States as Defendant

The Atomic Testing Liability Act is only one of many statutes that substitute the United States as the defendant in place of a private entity or person in suits arising under state tort law. The Federal Tort Claims Act itself immunizes federal employees from suits under state tort law for acts committed within the scope of employment. 28 U.S.C. § 2679(b)(1). The National Swine Flu Immunization Program of 1976, P.L. 94-380, made the United States liable for injuries arising out of the administration of the swine flu vaccine to the extent that vaccine manufacturers or distributors would be liable under state law, though it allowed the United States, if it paid any claim, to sue a vaccine manufacturer or distributor whose negligent conduct had caused the injury giving rise to such claim.[62]

Congress has also enacted more than 50 statutes that provide that various non-federal individuals or entities shall be treated as federal employees for purposes of liability.[63] These statutes generally apply to volunteers with various federal programs, including federally funded medical clinics and their officers and employees, "free clinic health professionals,"[64] members and personnel of the National Gambling Impact Study Commission, Peace Corps volunteers, and volunteers under the Volunteers in the National Forests Act of 1972 and the

Volunteers in the Parks Act of 1969. A recent enactment of this type of provision was section 304 of the Homeland Security Act of 2002, Public Law 107-296, which treats manufacturers and administrators of smallpox vaccine as federal employees for liability purposes.

Volunteers and entities covered by these statutes and others may not be sued for torts committed within the scope of their employment, but victims of their negligence may sue the United States under the Federal Tort Claims Act. The United States' liability, however, is limited in various ways. The United States may not, for example, be held liable for discretionary functions (i.e., policy decisions), or for punitive damages.

National Childhood Vaccine Injury Compensation Act of 1986 42 U.S.C. §§ 300aa-1 to 300aa-34

This statute prohibits suits under state tort law against manufacturers and administrators of specified vaccines unless the claimant first files a claim for limited (e.g., $250,000 cap on pain and suffering) no-fault compensation with the National Vaccine Injury Compensation Program, which is "administered by a Director selected by the Secretary" of Health and Human Services. Claims are adjudicated by the United States Court of Federal Claims and are paid by the Vaccine Injury Compensation Trust Fund, which is funded by a tax on vaccines.

A claimant dissatisfied with recovery under the Program may sue under state tort law, but the statute imposes various limitations on such suits; for example, manufacturers are not liable for failure to provide warnings directly to the injured party, as warnings to the person administering the vaccine are made sufficient. 42 U.S.C. § 300aa-22(c).

Comprehensive Environmental Response, Compensation, and Liability Act (Superfund)

This statute overrides state tort law in sections 112(e) and 309(a), 42 U.S.C. §§ 9612(e) and 9658(a). Section 112(e) provides that, "[r]egardless of any State statutory or common law to the contrary," no person who asserts a claim against the Fund shall be deemed to have waived any other claim arising from the same transaction. Section 309(a) provides that, "[i]n the case of any action brought under State law for personal injury, or property damages, which are caused or contributed to by exposure to any hazardous substance if the applicable limitations period for such action (as specified in the State statute of limitations or under common law) provides a commencement date which is earlier than the federally required commencement date," then the federally required commencement date shall govern.

General Aviation Revitalization Act, P.L. 103-298 (1994), 49 U.S.C. § 40101 Note

P.L. 103-298 bars any products liability suit against a manufacturer involving planes more than 18 years old with fewer than 20 seats that are not used in scheduled service.

Cruise Ship Liability, P.L. 104-324, § 1129 (1996)

This section of the Coast Guard Authorization Act of 1996 (P.L. 104-324) added 46 U.S.C. App. § 183(g):

> In a suit by any person in which the operator or owner of a vessel or employer of a crewmember is claimed to have vicarious liability for medical malpractice with regard to a crewmember occurring at a shoreside facility such operator, owner, or employer shall be entitled to rely upon any and all statutory limitations of liability in the State of the United States in which the shoreside medical care was provided.

Section 1129 also added 46 U.S.C. App. § 183c(b) to allow:

> contracts, agreements, or ticket conditions of carriage with passengers which relieve a crewmember, manager, agent, master, owner, or operator of a vessel from liability for infliction of emotional distress, mental suffering, or psychological injury

Such liability, however, may not be limited if the emotional distress, mental suffering, or psychological injury was the result of physical injury to the claimant or the result of the claimant's having been at actual risk of physical injury, if such injury or risk was caused by the negligence or fault of a crewmember or the manager, agent, master, owner, or operator. Such liability also may not be limited if it the emotional distress, mental suffering, or psychological injury was intentionally inflicted, or involved sexual harassment, sexual assault, or rape by a crewmember or the manager, agent, master, owner, or operator.

Bill Emerson Good Samaritan Food Donation Act, P.L. 104-210 (1996), 42 U.S.C. § 1791

P.L. 104-2 10 provides that a person ("an individual, corporation, partnership, organization, association, or governmental entity") or a gleaner ("a person who harvests for free distribution to the needy"), except in cases of gross negligence or intentional misconduct, "shall not be subject to civil or criminal liability arising from the nature, age, packaging, or condition of apparently wholesome food or an apparently fit grocery product that the person or gleaner donates in good faith to a non-profit organization for ultimate distribution to needy individuals." The nonprofit organization that receives the donation shall also not be liable, except in cases of gross negligence or intentional misconduct. The statute defines "gross negligence" as "voluntary and conscious conduct (including a failure to act) by a person who, at the time of the conduct, knew that the conduct was likely to be harmful to the health or well-being of another person." The *Federal Food Donation Act of 2008,* P.L. 110-247, provides that "all [federal] contracts above $25,000 for the provision, service, or sale of food in the United States, or for the lease or rental of Federal property to a private entity for events at which food is provided in the United States, shall include a clause that" states, "An executive agency (including an executive agency that enters into a contract with a contractor) and any contractor making donations pursuant to this Act [P.L. 110-247] shall be exempt from civil and criminal liability to the extent provided under the Bill Emerson Good Samaritan Food Donation Act (42 U.S.C. 1791)." As federal agencies and contractors are already covered by the Bill Emerson Good Samaritan Food Donation Act, the effect of the 2008 statute is to alert contractors to that fact.

Volunteer Protection Act of 1997, P.L. 105-19 (1997) , 42 U.S.C. §§ 14501-14505

P.L. 105-19 provides immunity for ordinary negligence to volunteers for nonprofit organizations or governmental entities acting within the scope of their responsibilities, provided that, "if appropriate or required, the volunteer was properly licensed, certified, or authorized by the appropriate authorities " The immunity does not apply to "willful or criminal conduct, gross negligence, reckless misconduct, or a conscious, flagrant indifference to the rights or safety of the individual harmed by the volunteer." This liability limitation does *not* apply to nonprofit organizations or governmental entities; they may be held vicariously liable for the ordinary negligence of their volunteers, even if volunteers are immune. Nonprofit organizations and governmental entities, however, may continue to benefit from any liability limitations provided by state law.

The Volunteer Protection Act of 1997 also eliminates joint and several liability for noneconomic damages with respect to volunteers' work for nonprofit organizations and governmental entities, and allows punitive damages only where the plaintiff establishes "by clear and convincing evidence that the harm was proximately caused by an action of such volunteer which constitutes willful or criminal misconduct, or a conscious, flagrant indifference to the rights or safety of the individual harmed."

The Volunteer Protection Act of 1997 preempts inconsistent state laws except to the extent that such laws provide additional protection from liability to volunteers, nonprofit organizations, or governmental entities. In addition, it allows states to enact statutes "declaring the election of such State that this Act shall not apply to such civil action in the State." If they do so, then the statute would not apply in any action if all parties to the action are citizens of the state.

Amtrak Reform and Accountability Act of 1997, P.L. 105-134, § 161 (1997), 49 U.S.C. § 28103

P.L. 105-134 limits damages in rail accidents. It permits punitive damages to be awarded, to the extent permitted by applicable state law, "only if the plaintiff establishes by clear and convincing evidence that the harm that is the subject of the action was the result of conduct carried out by the defendant with a conscious, flagrant indifference to the rights or safety of others." It also provides: "The aggregate allowable awards to all rail passengers, against all defendants, for all claims, including claims for punitive damages, arising from a single accident or incident, shall not exceed $200,000,000."

Aviation Medical Assistance Act of 1998, P.L. 105-170 (1998), 49 U.S.C. § 44701 Note

P.L. 105-170, § 5, provides that an air carrier shall not be liable for damages "arising out of the performance of the air carrier in obtaining or attempting to obtain the assistance of a passenger in an in-flight medical emergency, or out of the acts or omissions of the passenger rendering the assistance, if the passenger is not an employee or agent of the carrier and the carrier in good faith believes that the passenger is a medically qualified individual."

This statute also immunizes an individual in the above circumstances "unless the individual, while rendering such assistance, is guilty of gross negligence or willful misconduct."

Biomaterials Access Assurance Act of 1998, P.L. 105-230 (1998), 21 U.S.C. §§ 1601-1 606

P.L. 105-230 limits the products liability under state law of biomaterials suppliers, which it defines as "an entity that directly or indirectly supplies a component part or raw material for use in the manufacture of an implant." A biomaterials supplier may be held liable under state law only if it is the manufacturer of the implant; if it is the seller of the implant in certain limited situations; or, if it is neither the manufacturer nor seller of the implant, then only if it supplied raw materials or component parts for use in the implant that either did not constitute the product described in the contract or failed to meet specifications as provided in the statute. The statute also contains special procedures for the dismissal of civil actions against biomaterials suppliers.

Y2K Act, P.L. 106-37 (1999), 15 U.S.C. §§ 6601-6617

P.L. 106-37 limits contractual and tort liability under state law in suits, other than those for personal injury or wrongful death, "in which the plaintiff's alleged harm or injury arises from or is related to an actual or potential Y2K failure " Limitations on tort liability include (1) a cap on punitive damages, of the lesser of three times the amount awarded for compensatory damages or $250,000, but the cap applies only to defendants who are individuals whose net worth does not exceed $500,000 or organizations with fewer than 50 full-time employees, (2) a "clear and convincing evidence" standard for the recovery of punitive damages,

(3) the elimination of joint and several liability except in cases of specific intent to injure or knowing commission of fraud, and except in some cases in which damages against a defendant are uncollectible, and (4) except in the case of an "intentional tort arising independent of a contract," a prohibition on damages for economic loss, including lost profits or sales.

Cardiac Arrest Survival Act of 2000, P.L. 106-505, § 404 (2000), 42 U.S.C. § 238q

P.L. 106-505 provides good Samaritan protections regarding automated external defibrillators (AEDs). It provides that, with exceptions, "any person who uses or attempts to use an automated external defibrillator device on a victim of a perceived medical emergency is immune from civil liability; and in addition, any person who acquired the device is immune from such liability," except in specified circumstances.

A defendant shall not have immunity under this statute if the defendant (1) commits willful or criminal misconduct or gross negligence, (2) is a licensed or certified health professional acting within the scope of employment or agency, (3) is a hospital or clinic whose employee or agent used the AED while acting within the scope of employment or agency, or (4) is an acquirer of the AED who leased it to a health care entity, and the harm was caused by an employee or agent of the entity.

This statute supersedes state law only to the extent that a state has no statute or regulations that provide persons within the class protected by this statute with immunity for civil liability arising from the use of AEDs.

Air Transportation Safety and System Stabilization Act, 49 U.S.C. § 44303(b)

This statute provides that, "[f]or acts of terrorism committed on or to an air carrier during the period beginning on September 22, 2001, and ending on December 31, 2008, the Secretary [of Transportation] may certify that the air carrier was a victim of an act of terrorism and shall not be responsible for losses suffered by third parties (as referred to in section 205.5(b)(1) of title 14, Code of Federal Regulations) that exceed $100,000,000, in the aggregate, for all claims by such parties arising out of such act." If the Secretary so certifies, making the air carrier not liable for an amount that exceeds $100 million, then "the Government shall be responsible for any liability above such amount. No punitive damages may be awarded against an air carrier (or the Government taking responsibility for an air carrier under this subsection) under a cause of action arising out of such act."

This statute was enacted by P.L. 107-42, § 201(b), and sunset on March 21, 2002. It has been extended, however, most recently by P.L. 110-161, Div. K, § 114(b), 121 Stat. 2381 (2007), through 2008. The section in the Code of Federal Regulations that § 201(b) mentions refers to "persons, including non-employee cargo attendants, other than passengers"; these are apparently the "third parties" to whom § 20 1(b) refers.

September 11th Victim Compensation Fund of 2001, 49 U.S.C. § 40101 Note

P.L. 107-42, Title IV, as amended, created a federal program to compensate victims of the September 11, 2001 terrorist attacks. A victim or the victim's estate may seek no-fault compensation from the program or may bring a tort action against an airline or any other party, but may not do both, except that a victim or the victim's estate may recover under the program and also sue "any person who is a knowing participant in any conspiracy to hijack an aircraft or commit any terrorist act." The number of people who may recover by way of lawsuits may be limited, however, as the statute limits the liability of air carriers (including air transportation security companies and their affiliates), aircraft manufacturers, airport sponsors, or persons with an interest in the World Trade Center on September 11, 2001, to the limits of their liability insurance coverage. The statute gives the United States a right of subrogation with respect to any claim it pays under the compensation program. This means that the United States can recover amounts it pays under the compensation program from any party whom the victim could sue (i.e., a terrorist) or would have been able to sue had she or he not filed a claim under the program. The United States' subrogation rights, however, are limited to the caps mentioned above.

On March 7, 2002, the Department of Justice issued its final rule implementing the September 11th Victim Compensation Fund.[65] The final day to file a claim under the fund was December 22, 2003.

Paul D. Coverdell Teacher Protection Act of 2001, P.L. 107-110, §§ 2361-2368

P.L. 107-110 limits the liability of teachers, which it defines to include instructors, principals, administrators, members of a school board, and other educational professionals or nonprofessionals who work in a school and who are called on to maintain discipline or ensure safety. The liability limitations, however, apply only in states that receive funds under "this Act" (apparently P.L. 107-110) and that do not enact a statute declaring that the act shall not apply in the state.

The act provides that no teacher shall be liable for ordinary negligence in performing actions that are legal and "in furtherance of efforts to control discipline, expel, or suspend a student or maintain order or control in the classroom or school." A teacher may be liable for "willful or criminal misconduct, gross negligence, reckless misconduct, or a conscious, flagrant indifference to the rights or safety of the individual harmed by the teacher." The act does not limit liability for harm caused by a teacher operating a motor vehicle, vessel, aircraft, or other vehicle for which the state requires an operator or owner to possess an operator's license or to maintain insurance, and it does not apply "to misconduct during background investigations, or during other actions, involved in the hiring of a teacher."

In cases in which a teacher may be held liable, punitive damages may not be awarded "unless the claimant establishes by clear and convincing evidence that the harm was proximately caused by willful or criminal misconduct, or a conscious flagrant indifference to the rights or safety of the individual harmed." In addition, joint and several liability shall not apply to noneconomic damages.

Multiparty, Multiforum Trial Jurisdiction Act of 2002, P.L. 107-273, § 11020

P.L. 107-273, at 28 U.S C. § 1369, provides that, under specified circumstances, federal "district courts shall have original jurisdiction of any civil action involving minimal diversity between adverse parties that arises from a single accident, where at least 75 natural persons have died in the accident at a discrete location."[66]

Homeland Security Act of 2002, P.L. 107-296, §§ 304, 863, 890, 1201, 1402, and 1714-1717

P.L. 107-296 includes six different tort liability provisions (some mentioned as amendments to statutes listed above), which limit the liability of, respectively, smallpox vaccine manufacturers and administrators, sellers of anti-terrorism technology (the SAFETY Act), air transportation security companies and their affiliates, air carriers, Federal flight deck officers, and manufacturers and administrators of components and ingredients of various vaccines.[67] This last liability limitation — an amendment to the National Childhood Vaccine Injury Act of 1986, which appeared in §§ 1714-1717 of the Homeland Security Act of 2002 — was repealed by Public Law 108-7, Division L, § 102.

SAFETY Act, P.L. 107-296, § 863

The Support Anti-terrorism by Fostering Effective Technologies Act of 2002, or the SAFETY Act, (P.L. 107-296), is one of the tort liability provisions in the Homeland Security of 2002. Section 863 created a federal cause of action against sellers of anti-terrorism technologies for claims arising out of "an act of terrorism when qualified anti-terrorism technologies have been deployed in defense against or recovery from such act. " This federal cause of action preempts state tort law and provides for more limited liability than does state tort law; for example, it prohibits punitive damages, joint and several liability for noneconomic damages, and use of the collateral source rule. The federal cause of action applies only to technology approved by the Secretary of Homeland Security.[68]

PROTECT Act, P.L. 108-21, § 305

Section 305 of the Prosecutorial Remedies and Other Tools to end the Exploitation of Children Today Act of 2003, or the PROTECT Act (P.L. 108-21), provides that neither the National Center for Missing and Exploited Children, nor any of its officers, employees, or agents, shall "be liable for damages in any civil action for defamation, libel, slander, or harm to reputation arising out of any action or communication," unless it or he or she "acted with actual malice, or provided information or took action for a purpose unrelated to an activity mandated by Federal law."

Class Action Fairness Act of 2005, P.L. 109-2

P.L. 109-2, which is not applicable only to tort actions, amended 28 U.S.C. § 1332 to provide that the federal district courts shall have exclusive jurisdiction over any class action in which the matter in controversy exceeds $5 million and any member of a class of plaintiffs is a citizen of a state different from any defendant.

Among the statute's other provisions is a new 28 U.S.C. § 1453 to govern removal of class actions from state court to federal district court.[69]

Protection of Lawful Commerce in Arms Act, P.L. 109-92 (2005)

P.L. 109-92 prohibits "a civil action or proceeding or an administrative proceeding," except in six circumstances, against a manufacturer or seller of a firearm or ammunition, or a trade association, for damages "resulting from the criminal or unlawful misuse" of a firearm or ammunition. The exceptions cause the statute not to bar suits if, among other circumstances, the defendant violated a statute or engaged in negligent entrustment or an act of negligence per se. One of the exceptions ensures that the Bureau of Alcohol, Tobacco, Firearms and Explosives may still bring proceedings against gun manufacturers and sellers.

Section 5 of P.L. 109-92 is a separate law called the Child Safety Lock Act of 2005. With exceptions, it requires a "secure gun storage or safety device" (as defined in 18 U.S.C. § 921(a)(34)) on handguns, and provides that a person who has lawful possession and control of a handgun, and who uses such a device, is entitled to the same immunity as granted to gun manufacturers, sellers, and trade associations by P.L. 109-92.[70]

Public Readiness and Emergency Preparedness Act, P.L. 109-148, Division C (2005)

P.L. 109-148 limits liability with respect to pandemic flu and other public health countermeasures. Upon a declaration by the Secretary of Health and Human Services of a public health emergency or the credible risk of such emergency, the statute would, with respect to a "covered countermeasure," eliminate liability, with one exception, for the United States, and for manufacturers, distributors, program planners, persons who prescribe, administer or dispense the countermeasure, and employees of any of the above. The exception would be that a defendant who engaged in willful misconduct would be subject to liability under a new federal cause of action, though not under state tort law. However, victims could, in lieu of suing, accept payment under a new "Covered Countermeasure Process Fund," if Congress appropriates money for this fund.[71]

The Adam Walsh Child Protection and Safety Act of 2006, P.L. 109-248

The Protection of Children From Sexual Predators Act of 1998, P.L. 105-3 14, § 604, added § 227 to the Victims of Child Abuse Act of 1990, 42 U.S.C. §§ 13001 *et seq*. Section 227(b)(1), 42 U.S.C. § 13032(b)(1), provides that

> Whoever, while engaged in providing an electronic communication service or a remote computing service to the public, through a facility or means of interstate or foreign commerce, obtains knowledge of facts or circumstances from which a violation of [a specified federal child pornography statute], is apparent, shall, as soon as reasonably possible, make a report of such facts or circumstances to the Cyber Tip Line at the National Center for Missing and Exploited Children, which shall forward that report to a law enforcement agency or agencies designated by the Attorney General.

The Adam Walsh Child Protection and Safety Act of 2006, P.L. 109-248, § 130, added 42 U.S.C. § 13032(g), which grants the National Center for Missing and Exploited Children, as well as its directors, officers, employees, or agents, immunity from civil or criminal liability arising from the performance of Cyber Tip Line responsibilities, except when the Center or any of the above individuals engages in intentional misconduct or reckless disregard to a substantial risk of causing injury without legal justification.

Implementing Recommendations of the 9/11 Commission Act of 2007, 6 U.S.C. § 1104(c)

P.L. 110-53, § 1206 (2007), provides immunity from liability to people who, "in good faith and based on objectively reasonable suspicion," report to an authorized official suspicious activity regarding "a passenger transportation system or vehicle or its passengers." The statute also provides, "Any authorized official who observes, or receives a report of, covered activity and takes reasonable action in good faith to respond to such activity shall have qualified immunity from civil liability for such action, consistent with applicable law in the relevant jurisdiction. An authorized official not entitled to assert the defense of qualified immunity shall nevertheless be immune from civil liability under Federal, State, and local law if such authorized official takes reasonable action, in good faith, to respond to the reported activity."

FISA Amendments Act of 2008

Title I of P.L. 110-261, the Foreign Intelligence Surveillance Act Amendments Act of 2008, contains two prospective immunity provisions for electronic communication service providers. Title I defines electronic communication service providers as telecommunications carriers, providers of electronic communication services and remote computing services, and "any other communication service provider who has access to wire or electronic communications either as such communications are transmitted or as such communications are stored," as well as

the officers, employees, and agents of such entities.[72] First, the statute provides that "[n]o cause of action shall lie in any court against any electronic communication service provider for providing any information, facilities, or assistance in accordance with a directive issued"[73] by the Attorney General and the Director of National Intelligence, after a Foreign Intelligence Surveillance Court (FISC) order or a determination of exigent circumstances, in connection with the targeting of non- United States persons "reasonably believed to be located outside of the United States to acquire foreign intelligence information."[74] Second, the statute further provides that "[n]o cause of action shall lie in any court against any electronic communication service provider for providing any information, facilities, or assistance in accordance with" a FISC order or request for emergency assistance in connection with the targeting of a United States person reasonably believed to be located outside the United States to gather foreign intelligence information.[75]

Title II of P.L. 110-261 provides for the dismissal of certain pending civil actions against any "person," which the act defines to include electronic communication service providers as well as "a landlord, custodian, or other person who may be authorized or required to furnish assistance pursuant to" certain orders of the FISC, certifications, or directives.[76] Such actions must be dismissed if the United States district court finds substantial evidence to support the Attorney General's certification that any assistance provided by that person fit within one of five categories listed in § 802(a) of the FISA Act of 1978, as amended by P.L. 110- 261.[77] State court civil actions would be removable to federal court.[78]

ENDNOTES

[1] In addition, under its power to spend for the "general Welfare of the United States" (Art. I, § 8, cl. 1), Congress may require the states to implement tort reform as a condition of their acceptance of federal funds. South Dakota v. Dole, 483 U.S. 203, 206 (1987) (Congress "may attach conditions on the receipt of federal funds, and has repeatedly employed the power 'to further broad policy objectives by conditioning receipt of federal moneys with compliance by the recipient with federal statutory and administrative directives'").

[2] In *United States v. Lopez*, 514 U.S. 549, 559 (1995), the Supreme Court made clear that, to be subject to federal regulation, an activity must "substantially affect" and not merely "affect" interstate commerce.

[3] This power enables Congress to regulate noncommercial activities that cross state lines. Thus, in *Caminetti v. United States*, 242 U.S. 470 (1917), the Court upheld a federal statute that it a crime knowingly to transport in interstate commerce "any woman or girl for the purpose of prostitution or debauchery, or for any other immoral purpose," even though the statute, as interpreted by the Court, was not limited to "commercialized vice." *Id.* at 484.

[4] The Court added: "While we need not adopt a categorical rule against aggregating the effects of any noneconomic activity in order to decide these cases, thus far in our Nation's history our cases have upheld Commerce Clause regulation of intrastate activity only where that activity is economic in nature." *Id.* at 613. By contrast, the Court will uphold Commerce Clause regulation of *interstate* activity that is not economic in nature; see note 3, *supra*.

[5] Fein v. Permanente Medical Group, 38 Cal.3d 137, 211 Cal. Rptr. 368, 695 P.2d 665 (1985), *appeal dismissed*, 474 U.S. 892 (1985) (Justice White dissenting); Roa v. Lodi Medical Group, Inc., 37 Cal.3d 920, 211 Cal. Rptr. 77, 695 P.2d 164 (1985), *appeal dismissed*, 474 U.S. 990 (1985).

[6] 426 U.S. at 843, quoting *Fry v. United States*, 421 U.S. 542, 547 n.7 (1975). The Tenth Amendment states: "The powers not delegated to the United States by

the Constitution, nor prohibited by it to the States, are reserved to the States respectively, or to the people."

7 Subsequently, in *Printz v. United States*, 521 U.S. 898, 935 (1997), the Court held that Congress may not "circumvent" the prohibition on commandeering a state's regulatory processes "by conscripting the State's officers directly."

8 "[W]hen Congress creates new statutory 'public rights,' it may assign their adjudication to an administrative agency with which a jury trial would be incompatible, without violating the Seventh Amendment's injunction that jury trial is to be 'preserved' in 'suits at common law.'" Granfinanciera, S.A. v. Nordberg, 492 U.S. 33, 51 (1989).

9 Suits based on state law may be brought in federal court only if the matter in controversy exceeds $75,000 and the plaintiff and defendant are domiciled in different states. This is known as "diversity of citizenship." 28 U.S.C. § 1332.

10 "The constitutions of 48 states have civil jury provisions roughly analogous in form and substance to the seventh amendment." Paul B. Weiss, *Reforming Tort Reform: Is There Substance to the Seventh Amendment?*, 38 Catholic University Law Review 737, 739 (1989).

11 Simler v. Connor, 372 U.S. 221 (1963).

12 "Common law" refers to law created by state courts, on a case-by-case basis.

13 This does not mean that juries must operate exactly as they did at common law. In *Colgrove v. Battin*, 413 U.S. 149 (1973), the Supreme Court upheld rules adopted in a federal district court authorizing civil juries composed of six persons. By the reference in the Seventh Amendment to the "common law," the Court wrote, "the Framers of the Seventh Amendment were concerned with preserving the *right* of trial by jury in civil cases where it existed at common law, rather than the various incidents of trial by jury." *Id.* at 155-156 (emphasis in original). Presumably, allowing a less than unanimous verdict would also be permissible, even though a unanimous verdict was required at common law.

14 Minneapolis & St. Louis R.R. Co. v. Bombolis, 241 U.S. 211 (1916). The Seventh Amendment does apply in District of Columbia courts. Capital Traction Co. v. Hof, 174 U.S. 1, 5 (1899).

15 Simler v. Connor, *supra* note 11.

16 Congress, pursuant to the Constitution (Art. III, § 1) "may from time to time ordain and establish," and hence limit the jurisdiction of, "inferior" federal courts. (Art. I, § 3, directly establishes the Supreme Court.)

17 *See* 5 U.S.C. § 8116(c) (United States' liability under FECA is exclusive); 28 U.S.C. § 2679(b)(1) (federal employees are immune from tort actions arising under state law).

[18] Mountain Timber Co. v. Washington, 243 U.S. 219, 235 (1917).

[19] Whether Congress may require the use of non-federally established arbitration panels is considered in Section F, below.

[20] Palmore v. United States, 411 U.S. 389, 408 (1973).

[21] 458 U.S. 50, 70 (1982).

[22] *Id.* at 64-70.

[23] *Id.* at 69-70 (emphasis in original; citations omitted).

[24] Thomas v. Union Carbide Agricultural Products Co., 473 U.S. 568, 586 (1985).

[25] 492 U.S. 33, 54-55 (1989) (citation omitted).

[26] *Id.* at 52 (emphasis in original; citations omitted).

[27] *Id.* at 53-54.

[28] Prohibiting states from using jury trials in tort cases, without establishing a federal forum to decide such cases, might be done in various ways, such as by requiring binding arbitration or by allowing ordinary state court trials but requiring that judges be factfinders.

[29] 473 U.S. 568, 584 (1985).

[30] In the National Childhood Vaccine Injury Act of 1986, as amended, 42 U.S.C. §§ 300aa-1 — 300aa-34, Congress required that vaccine-related injury claims be heard by a special master designated by the United States Claims Court. However, the statute both alters the traditional common law action to a no-fault claim with limited recovery, and allows a dissatisfied claimant to bring a traditional state tort action, with some modifications.

[31] 492 U.S. at 52, 54.

[32] 473 U.S. at 586.

[33] *Id.* at 587.

[34] *Id.* at 572.

[35] *Id.* at 573.

[36] *Id.* at 573-574.

[37] *Id.* at 584.

[38] *Id.* at 589.

[39] 492 U.S. at 54.

[40] 473 U.S. at 591.

[41] *Id.* at 592.

[42] 478 U.S. 833, 851 (1986) (citations omitted).

[43] *Id.*

[44] *Id.* at 852.

[45] *Id.* at 853.

[46] 458 U.S. at 71.

[47] *Id.* at 77.

[48] *Id.* at 85.
[49] 492 U.S. at 55-56.
[50] *Id.* at 60-61.
[51] *Id.* at 61 (citations omitted).
[52] *Id.* at 63.
[53] 473 U.S. at 589.
[54] 478 U.S. at 851.
[55] *Id.* at 857.
[56] In *Kline v. Wheels by Kinney, Inc.*, 464 F.2d 184, 187 (4th Cir. 1972), a federal court wrote: "With no North Carolina case directly on point, our judicial chore is to 'determine the rule that the North Carolina Supreme Court would probably follow, not fashion a rule which we, as an independent federal court, might consider best.'"
[57] Wright & Miller, *Federal Practice And Procedure* : Civil § 2303.
[58] Hart, *The Relations Between State and Federal Law*, 54 Columbia Law Review 489, 508 (1954). The Supreme Court has qualified this rule, writing: "Federal law takes state courts as it finds them only insofar as those courts employ rules that do not 'impose unnecessary burdens upon rights of recovery authorized by federal laws.'" Felder v. Casey, 487 U.S. 131, 150 (1988). However, federal rights of recovery would not be at issue if Congress sought to eliminate jury trials of state tort claims, and the Court's qualification would be irrelevant in such a case.
[59] Missouri ex rel. Southern Railway Co. v. Mayfield, 340 U.S. 1, 4 (1950). The Court continued, however: "No such restriction is imposed upon the States merely because the Employers' Liability Act empowers their courts to entertain suits arising under it," thus not addressing the issue of the constitutionality of Congress' imposing such a restriction.
[60] As it happened, because of exceptions in the Federal Tort Claims Act, the United States could not be held liable, and Congress as a consequence enacted the Radiation Exposure Compensation Act, 42 U.S C. § 2210 note, a compensation program for individuals exposed to radiation between specified dates in 1951 and 1962.
[61] *In re* Consolidated United States Atmospheric Testing Litigation, 820 F.2d 982 (9th Cir. 1987), *cert. denied*, 485 U.S. 905 (1988); Hammond v. United States, 786 F.2d 8 (1st Cir. 1986).
[62] The Swine Flu law made the United States liable not only for the negligence but for the strict liability of manufacturers and distributors, even though the United States ordinarily may not be held strictly liable under the Federal Tort Claims Act, regardless of state law.

[63] Many of these statutes are listed in CRS Report 97-579, *Making Private Entities and Individuals Immune from Tort Liability by Declaring them Federal Employees*, by Henry Cohen.

[64] For additional information on these first two categories, see CRS Report RS20984, *Public Health Service Act Provisions Providing Immunity from Medical Malpractice Liability*, by Henry Cohen.

[65] 28 C.F.R. Part 104 [http://www.usdoj.gov/final_report.pdf]. For additional information on this statute and the Department of Justice's implementation of it, see CRS Report RL3 1179, *The September 11th Victim Compensation Fund of 2001*, by Henry Cohen.

[66] For additional information, see CRS Report RS20861, *Multiparty, Multiforum Trial Jurisdiction Act of 2002, P.L. 107-2 73*, by Paul Starett Wallace Jr. and Mark Gurevitz.

[67] All six provisions are examined in CRS Report RL3 1649, *Homeland Security Act of 2002: Tort Liability Provisions*, by Henry Cohen.

[68] Department of Homeland Security regulations implementing the SAFETY Act appear at 6 C.F.R. Part 25.

[69] For additional information, see CRS Report RL32761, *Class Actions and Legislative Proposals in the 109th Congress: Class Action Fairness Act of 2005*, by Paul Starett Wallace Jr.

[70] For additional information, see CRS Report RS22074, *Limiting Tort Liability of Gun Manufacturers and Gun Sellers: Legal Analysis of P.L. 109-92 (2005)*, by Henry Cohen.

[71] For additional information, see CRS Report RS22327, *Pandemic Flu and Medical Biodefense Countermeasure Liability Legislation: P.L. 109-148, Division C (2005)*, by Henry Cohen and Vanessa K. Burrows.

[72] P.L. 110-261, § 101 (creating § 701 (b)(4) of the Foreign Intelligence Surveillance Act of 1978, as amended (FISA Act)).

[73] P.L. 110-261, § 101 (creating § 702(h)(3) of the FISA Act).

[74] P.L. 110-261, § 101 (creating § 702(a) of the FISA Act).

[75] P.L. 110-261, § 101 (amending § 703(e) of the FISA Act).

[76] P.L. 110-261, § 201 (creating §§ 801, 802 of the FISA Act).

[77] P.L. 110-261, § 201 (creating § 802(a), (b)(1) of the FISA Act).

[78] P.L. 110-261, § 201 (creating § 802(g) of the FISA Act). For additional information, see CRS Report RL34279, *The Foreign Intelligence Surveillance Act: An Overview of Selected Issues*, by Elizabeth B. Bazan, and CRS Report RL34566, *The Foreign Intelligence Surveillance Act: A Sketch of Selected Issues*, by Elizabeth B. Bazan.

In: Federal Torts Reform, Claims and Liability ISBN 978-1-60692-989-6
Editor: Ben V. Colligan

Chapter 2

FEDERAL TORT CLAIMS ACT*

Henry Cohen and Vanessa K. Burrows

SUMMARY

The Federal Tort Claims Act is the statute by which the United States authorizes tort suits to be brought against itself. With exceptions, it makes the United States liable for injuries caused by the negligent or wrongful act or omission of any federal employee acting within the scope of his employment, in accordance with the law of the state where the act or omission occurred. Three major exceptions, under which the United States may not be held liable, even in circumstances where a private person could be held liable under state law, are the *Feres* doctrine, which prohibits suits by military personnel for injuries sustained incident to service; the discretionary function exception, which immunizes the United States for acts or omissions of its employees that involve policy decisions; and the intentional tort exception, which precludes suits against the United States for assault and battery, among some other intentional torts, unless they are committed by federal law enforcement or investigative officials.

This chapter discusses, among other things, the application of the *Feres* doctrine to suits for injuries caused by medical malpractice in the military, the prohibition of suits by victims of atomic testing, Supreme Court cases interpreting the discretionary function exception, the extent to which federal employees may

* This is an edited, excerpted and augmented edition of a Congressional Research Service Report for Congress publication, Order Code 95-717, dated September 2, 2008.

be held liable for torts they commit in the scope of their employment, and the government contractor defense to products liability design defect suits.

In the 110th Congress, two bills have been introduced that would amend the Federal Tort Claims Act: H.R. 2249, the Federal Tort Claim Reform Act of 2007, and H.R. 6093, the Carmelo Rodriguez Military Medical Accountability Act of 2008.

INTRODUCTION

The Federal Tort Claims Act (FTCA), 28 U.S.C. §§ 1346(b), 2671-2680, is the statute by which the United States authorizes tort suits to be brought against itself. As a result of the common law doctrine of sovereign immunity, "the United States cannot be sued without its consent."[1] "Congress alone has the power to waive or qualify that immunity."[2] In 1946, by enacting the FTCA, Congress waived sovereign immunity for some tort suits. With exceptions, it made the United States liable:

> for injury or loss of property, or personal injury or death caused by the negligent or wrongful act or omission of any employee of the government while acting within the scope of his office or employment, under circumstances where the United States, if a private person would be liable to the claimant in accordance with the law of the place where the act or omission occurred.

28 U.S.C. § 1346(b).

Thus, the FTCA makes the United States liable for the torts of its employees[3] to the extent that private employers are liable under state law for the torts of their employees.[4] The fact that state law would make a state or municipal entity — as opposed to a *private* person — liable under like circumstances is not sufficient to make the United States liable under the FTCA.[5]

The FTCA, however, contains exceptions under which the United States may not be held liable even though a private employer could be held liable under state law. Three of these exceptions are examined in separate sections of this chapter: the *Feres* doctrine, which prohibits suits by military personnel for injuries sustained incident to service;[6] the discretionary function exception; and the intentional tort exception. Among the other exceptions, the United States may not be held liable in accordance with state law imposing strict liability;[7] it may not be held liable for interest prior to judgment or for punitive damages (28 U.S.C. § 2674);[8] for the act or omission of an employee exercising due care in the execution of an invalid statute or regulation (28 U.S.C. § 2680);[9] for claims "arising out of the loss, miscarriage, or negligent transmission of letters or postal matter";[10] for claims "arising in respect of the assessment or collection of any tax[11] or customs duty, or the detention of any goods, merchandise, or other property by any officer of customs or excise or any other law enforcement officer";[12] for claims caused by the fiscal operations of the Treasury or by the regulation of the monetary system; for claims arising out of combatant activities; or for claims arising in a foreign country.[13]

Prior to filing suit under the FTCA, a claimant must present his claim to the federal agency out of whose activities the claim arises. 28 U.S.C. § 2675.[14] This must be done within two years after the claim accrues. 28 U.S.C. § 2401.[15] If, within six months after receiving a claim, the agency mails a denial of the claim to the claimant, then the claimant has six months to file suit in federal district court. 28 U.S.C. §§ 2401, 2675. No period of limitations applies to a plaintiff if the agency fails to act within six months after receiving his claim.[16] Suits under the FTCA are tried without a jury. 28 U.S.C. § 2402.[17]

An agency may not settle a claim for more than $25,000 without the prior written approval of the Attorney General or his designee, unless the Attorney General delegates to the head of the agency the authority to do so.[18] "Such delegations may not exceed the authority delegated by the Attorney General to United States attorneys to settle claims for money damages against the United States."[19] United States attorneys are authorized to settle claims in amounts up to $1 million.[20] Settlements of $2,500 or less shall be paid by the agency out of appropriations available to the agency; settlements of more than $2,500 shall be paid from general revenues. 28 U.S.C. § 2672.

Attorneys who represent claimants under the FTCA may not charge claimants more than 25% of a court award or a settlement made by the Attorney General or his designee after suit is filed, or more than 20% of a settlement made by the agency with whom a claim is filed. 28 U.S.C. § 2678.[21] A court may not order the United States to pay a claimant's attorneys' fees unless the court finds the United States to have acted in bad faith. 28 U.S.C. § 2412(b).[22]

THE *FERES* DOCTRINE AND MEDICAL MALPRACTICE

In *Feres v. United States*, 340 U.S. 135 (1950), the Supreme Court unanimously held that, although the FTCA contains no explicit exclusion for injuries sustained by military personnel incident to service, such an exclusion results from construing the act "to fit, so far as will comport with its words, into the entire statutory scheme of remedies against the Government to make a workable, consistent and equitable whole." 340 U.S. at 139. One reason the Court found that to prohibit recovery for injuries sustained incident to service would fit the entire statutory scheme was that the act, at 28 U.S.C. § 2674, makes the United States liable only "to the same extent as a private individual under like circumstances." This limitation could be construed to exclude service-connected injuries because, the Court found,

> that plaintiffs can point to no liability of a "private individual" even remotely analogous to that which they are asserting against the United States. We know of no American law which ever has permitted a soldier to recover for negligence, against either his superior officers or the Government he is serving. Nor is there any liability "under like circumstances," for no private individual has power to conscript or mobilize a private army with such authorities over persons as the Government vests in echelons of command.

340 U.S. at 141-142.

Another basis for the Court's decision in *Feres* was that the act makes "the law of the place where the act or omission occurred" (28 U.S.C. § 1346(b)) govern liability, yet, in the case of a soldier, who is not free to choose his habitat, "[t]hat the geography of an injury should select the law to be applied to his tort claims makes no sense." *Id.* at 143. The Court also was influenced by the fact that Congress has enacted laws that "provide systems of simple, certain, and uniform compensation for injuries or death of those in armed services," yet Congress made no provision as to how recovery under the FTCA would affect entitlement to such compensation. "The absence of any such adjustment is persuasive that there was no awareness that the act might be interpreted to permit recovery for injuries incident to military service." *Id.* at 144. The Court concluded:

> that the Government is not liable under the Federal Tort Claims Act for injuries to servicemen where the injuries arise out of or are in the course of activity incident to service. Without exception, the relationship of military personnel to the Government has been governed exclusively by federal law. We do not think that Congress, in drafting the Act, created a new cause of action dependent on local law for service-connected injuries or death due to negligence. We cannot impute to Congress such a radical departure from established law in the absence of express congressional command.

340 U.S. at 146.

In *Stencel Aero Engineering Corp. v. United States*, 431 U.S. 666, 671-672 (1977), the Supreme Court identified three rationales as the foundation for the *Feres* doctrine:

> First, the relationship between the Government and members of its Armed Forces is "'distinctively federal in character,'"... ; it would make little sense to have the Government's liability to members of the Armed Services depend on the fortuity of where the soldier happened to be stationed at the time of the injury.
>
> Second, the Veterans' Benefits Act establishes as a substitute for tort liability, a statutory "no fault" compensation scheme which provides generous pensions to injured servicemen, without regard to any negligence attributable to the Government.
>
> A third factor was explicated in *United States v. Brown*, 348 U.S. 110, 112 (1954), namely, "[t]he peculiar and special relationship of the soldier to his superiors, the effects of the maintenance of such suits on discipline, and the extreme results that might obtain if suits under the Tort Claims Act were allowed for negligent orders given or negligent acts committed in the course of military duty ... ."

The Supreme Court reaffirmed the *Feres* doctrine in *United States v. Shearer*, 473 U.S. 52 (1985), and again addressed the reasons for its adoption. "*Feres* seems best explained," the Court wrote:

> "by the 'peculiar and special relationship of the soldier to his superiors, the effects of the maintenance of such suits on discipline, and the extreme results that might obtain if suits under the Tort Claims Act were allowed for negligent orders given or negligent acts committed in the course of military duty.'" The *Feres* doctrine cannot be reduced to a few bright-line rules; each case must be examined in light of the statute as it has been construed in *Feres* and subsequent cases.

473 U.S. at 57 (citations omitted).

The Court emphasized that significant factors in determining whether the *Feres* doctrine bars a suit are "whether the suit requires the civilian court to second-guess military decisions ... and whether the suit might impair military discipline." *Id.* at 57. It noted that "other factors mentioned in Feres" are "no longer controlling." *Id.* at 58 n.4. These other factors apparently were the distinctively federal nature of the relationship between the government and military personnel, and the alternative compensation system available to military personnel. Subsequently, however, in *United States v. Johnson*, 481 U.S. 681 (1987), discussed below, the Court reaffirmed these factors.

In *Atkinson v. United States*,[23] a panel of the United States Court of Appeals for the Ninth Circuit, relying primarily on *Shearer*, allowed a medical malpractice suit to be brought under the FTCA by a servicewoman who suffered injuries "incident to service" in an Army hospital. The government sought a rehearing, and, in the interim, the Supreme Court decided *United States v. Johnson*, *supra*, which caused the Ninth Circuit's panel to grant the rehearing and issue a new opinion in *Atkinson*, reversing itself. The Supreme Court subsequently declined to review the case. These three decisions — the panel's first decision in *Atkinson*, *Johnson*, and the panel's second decision in *Atkinson* — are now examined in turn.

The plaintiff in *Atkinson* alleged that negligence on the part of Army hospital personnel had caused her to deliver a stillborn child and to suffer physical and emotional injuries. The panel, in its first decision, wrote:

> [T]he *Feres* doctrine bars suit only where a civilian court would be called upon to second-guess military decisions or where the plaintiff's admitted activities are of the sort that would directly implicate the need to safeguard military discipline ... . In *Shearer*, the Supreme Court also confirmed that courts should take a case-by-case, rather than *per se*, approach to claims [by the government] of immunity.

804 F.2d at 563. Taking such an approach, the court wrote:

> At the time Atkinson sought treatment, she was "not subject in any real way to the compulsion of military orders or performing any sort of military mission."... . No command relationship exists between Atkinson and her attending physician. No military considerations govern the treatment in a non-field hospital of a woman who seeks to have a healthy baby. No military discipline applies to the care a conscientious physician will provide in this situation ... . There is simply no connection between Atkinson's medical treatment and the decisional or disciplinary interest protected by the *Feres* doctrine.

Id. at 564-565.

Note that this decision did not hold that all military malpractice suits are exempt from the *Feres* doctrine. In taking a case-by-case approach, the court allowed for the possibility of a situation in which there is a connection between a serviceman or servicewoman's "medical treatment and the decisional or disciplinary interest protected by the *Feres* doctrine."

In 1987, in *United States v. Johnson*, *supra*, the Supreme Court, in a 5-to-4 decision, held that the *Feres* doctrine bars suits on behalf of military personnel injured incident to service even in cases of torts committed by employees of civilian agencies. The plaintiff in *Johnson* was the widow of a serviceman killed incident to service in a helicopter crash allegedly caused by the negligence of the Federal Aviation Administration. Reexamining the reasons for the *Feres* doctrine, the Court concluded that whether the tortfeasor was a civilian or a military employee was not significant. The reasons for the *Feres* doctrine that it reexamined, and reaffirmed, were the three cited in *Stencel*, set forth on page 5 of this chapter. Thus, it removed any doubts that it had cast in *Shearer* upon the significance of those factors.

Justice Scalia, joined by three other justices in dissent, noted that the *Feres* doctrine is not in the FTCA as enacted by Congress, and found the reasons offered by the Court for adopting the doctrine to be unsatisfactory:

> [N]either the three original *Feres* reasons nor the post hoc rationalization of "military discipline" justifies our failure to apply the FTCA as written. *Feres* was wrongly decided and heartily deserves the "widespread, almost universal criticism" it has received.

481 U.S. at 700.[24]

Citing *Johnson*, the Ninth Circuit's panel subsequently reversed itself in *Atkinson*:

> Significant for our purposes [the panel wrote] is the Court's articulation, with apparent approval, of all three rationales associated with *Feres* ... . Simply put, *Johnson* appears to breathe new life into the first two *Feres* rationales, which until that time had been largely discredited and abandoned ... . Although we believe that the military discipline rationale does not support application of the *Feres* doctrine in this case, the first two rationales support its application ... . We are ... reluctant to carve out an exception to *Feres* after five members of the Court appear to have emphatically endorsed *Feres* and all three of its rationales. That task, if it is to be undertaken at all, is properly left to the Supreme Court or to Congress.

825 F.2d at 205-206.[25]

In *Del Rio v. United States*, 833 F.2d 282 (11th Cir. 1987), a servicewoman who had given birth to twins brought a medical malpractice suit under the FTCA, alleging that, as a result of negligent prenatal care at a military hospital, one of her twins suffered bodily injury and the other died. The Eleventh Circuit held that the *Feres* doctrine, as interpreted in *Johnson*, barred her claim. It agreed with the Ninth Circuit's second decision in *Atkinson* that the first two *Feres* factors operated to preclude suit, but, unlike the Ninth Circuit, believed that even the third factor did so. "Obviously," the court wrote, "the suit '*might* impair essential military discipline' ... ."[26]

In *Irvin v. United States*, 845 F.2d 126 (6th Cir. 1988), *cert. denied*, 488 U.S. 975 (1988), another servicewoman alleged that negligent prenatal care by the military had resulted in her infant's death, and another court of appeals held that the *Feres* doctrine barred suit under the FTCA.

In *Bowers v. United States*, 904 F.2d 450 (8th Cir. 1990), the court held that the *Feres* doctrine precludes an individual from recovering for medical malpractice allegedly committed at his pre-induction physical. Although the plaintiff was not a service member at the time of the alleged negligence, and was not eligible for either veterans' benefits or treatment in a military hospital, the court found that two of the three *Feres* rationales spelled out in *Johnson* were applicable: "the relationship between Bowers and the armed forces is distinctively federal," and a decision for Bowers "would have a direct effect upon military judgments and decisions." *Id.* at 452.

Thus, the *Feres* doctrine stands and contains no exception for medical malpractice cases. Because the first two *Stencel* factors — the federal nature of the relationship between the government and military personnel, and the alternative compensation scheme — would seem to apply in every case, there may not even be occasion for courts to use the case-by-case approach of *Shearer*. This could change, however, as a result of action by either the Supreme Court or Congress.

As for the Supreme Court, it is not beyond the realm of possibility that it could completely overrule *Feres*. In *Johnson*, as noted, the four dissenting justices said that *Feres* had been wrongly decided, and even downplayed the significance of the fact that Congress since 1950 has not overturned *Feres*. 481 U.S. at 702 (Scalia, J., dissenting). As for Congress, some Members in the past have shown interest in amending the *Feres* doctrine to the extent of authorizing medical malpractice suits.[27]

Although *Feres* was an interpretation of the FTCA, it has been applied to bar suits against the United States under other statutes, including the Privacy Act. *Cummings v. Department of Navy*, 116 F. Supp. 2d 76 (D.D.C. 2000).

The application of the *Feres* doctrine to spouses and children of military personnel is discussed below, at the beginning of the section on "Suits by Victims of Atomic Testing."

THE DISCRETIONARY FUNCTION EXCEPTION

The discretionary function exception is the most significant exception to government liability that is explicitly provided for in the FTCA. This exception immunizes the United States from claims "based upon the exercise or performance or the failure to exercise or perform a discretionary function." 28 U.S.C. § 2680(a). It precludes liability even if a federal employee acted negligently in the performance or nonperformance of his discretionary duty.[28] In *Dalehite v. United States*, 346 U.S. 15 (1953), the Supreme Court said that the discretion protected by the exception:

> is the discretion of the executive or administrator to act according to one's judgment of the best course .... It ... includes more than the initiation of programs and activities. It also includes determinations made by executives or administrators in establishing plans, specifications or schedules of operations. Where there is room for policy judgment and decision there is discretion. It necessarily follows that acts of subordinates in carrying out the operations of government in accordance with official directions cannot be actionable.

Id. at 34, 35-36 (footnotes omitted).

In *United States v. Varig Airlines*, 467 U.S. 797 (1984), victims of airplane accidents alleged that the Federal Aviation Administration (FAA) had acted negligently in certifying certain airplanes for operation. The FAA had established a program of "spot-checking" manufacturers' compliance with minimum safety standards, and had certified the airplanes involved in the accidents without inspecting them. The Supreme Court, applying the principles it had set forth in *Dalehite*, held:

> Here, the FAA has determined that a program of "spot-checking" manufacturers' compliance with minimum safety standards best accommodates the goal of air transportation safety and the reality of finite agency resources. Judicial intervention in such decisionmaking through private tort suits would require the courts to "second-guess" the political, social, and economic judgments of an agency exercising its regulatory function ... . It follows that the acts of FAA employees in executing the "spot-check" program in accordance

> with agency directives are protected by the discretionary function exception as well ... . The FAA employees who conducted compliance reviews of the aircraft involved in this case were specifically empowered to make policy judgments.

Id. at 820.[29]

In *Berkovitz v. United States*, 486 U.S. 531 (1988), the Supreme Court held that the United States could be held liable under the FTCA, because the plaintiffs had proved that federal employees had failed to follow regulations that specifically prescribed a course of action. The plaintiffs were an infant, who had contracted a severe case of polio from a dose of Orimune, an oral polio vaccine, and his parents. They claimed that the Division of Biologic Standards, then a part of the National Institutes of Health, had violated a federal statute and accompanying regulations in issuing a license to a vaccine manufacturer to produce Orimune, and that the Bureau of Biologics of the Food and Drug Administration had violated federal regulations in approving the release of the particular lot that contained the dose that injured the infant. The regulatory scheme governing licensing in *Berkovitz*, unlike the one challenged in *Varig*, did not permit spot-checking; it required the agency, "prior to issuing a product license, to receive all data the manufacturer is required to submit, examine the product, and make a determination that the product complies with safety standards." *Id.* at 542. The regulatory scheme governing release of vaccine lots apparently would have given the agency the power to establish a spot-checking program as was used in *Varig*. However, the plaintiffs alleged that the agency had:

> adopted a policy of testing all vaccine lots for compliance with safety standards and preventing the distribution to the public of any lots that fail to comply. [Plaintiffs] further allege that notwithstanding this policy, which allegedly leaves no room for implementing officials to exercise independent policy judgment, employees of the Bureau knowingly approved a lot that did not comply with safety standards.

Id. at 547.

The Court sent the case back for trial, holding that if these allegations were proved, then the discretionary function exception would not bar the claim.[30] The Court thus rejected the view expressed by the court below "that the discretionary function exception exempts the United States from claims based on ... non-discretionary operational level acts and omissions taken in furtherance of planning level discretionary decisions." 822 F.2d 1322, 1329 (3d Cir. 1987).

In *United States v. Gaubert*, 499 U.S. 315 (1991), the Court held that the discretionary function exception barred suit against the United States for the activities of federal bank regulators in connection with a failing savings and loan association, the Independent American Savings Association (IASA). The regulators became "involved in IASA's day-to-day business. They recommended the hiring of a certain consultant to advise IASA on operational and financial matters; they advised IASA concerning whether, when, and how its subsidiaries should be placed into bankruptcy; they mediated salary disputes; they reviewed the draft of a complaint to be used in litigation; they urged IASA to convert from state to federal charter; and they actively intervened when the Texas Savings and Loan Department attempted to install a supervisory agent at IASA." *Id.* at 3 19-320.

The plaintiff, who was IASA's chairman of the board and largest shareholder, alleged that these activities were performed negligently and cost him $100 million in damages. The United States argued that, even if the regulators' activities had been performed negligently, the discretionary function exception precluded recovery. The court of appeals found that only some of the regulators' activities were protected by the discretionary function exception: while "policy decisions" fall within the exception, "operational actions" do not. *Id.* at 321. The Supreme Court disagreed:

> A discretionary act is one that involves choice or judgment; there is nothing in that description that refers exclusively to policy-making or planning functions. Day-to-day management of banking affairs, like the management of other businesses, regularly require[s] judgment as to which of a range of permissible courses is the wisest.

Id. at 325.

The discretionary function exception thus applies to decisions based on policy, whether made at the policy or planning level, on the one hand, or at the operational level, on the other.[31]

SUITS BY VICTIMS OF ATOMIC TESTING

From 1946 to 1962, approximately 235 tests of atomic weapons were performed by federal government contractors. Many military and civilian personnel who participated in these tests claim to have suffered cancer and other long-term medical injuries as a result. Current federal law generally precludes either military or civilian personnel from recovering in tort against either the federal government or the contractors in these cases.

Military personnel are barred from recovering against the United States because of the *Feres* doctrine.

> The doctrine of the *Feres* case does not apply to the spouse or child of a serviceman insofar as their own injuries or death are concerned ... . Conversely, the *Feres* doctrine clearly bars a suit by a serviceman's next of kin for damages resulting from the death or of injuries to the serviceman if his death or injuries are incident to service.[32]

The distinction is between a spouse's or child's injury that is caused directly by the military and a spouse's or child's injury that results from the soldier's service-connected injury: the former is recoverable but the latter is not. Thus, courts of appeals have held that the *Feres* doctrine bars spouses of soldiers from recovering for their own injuries where such injuries resulted from the soldiers' injuries that were caused by the soldiers' having been ordered into nuclear blast areas.[33]

Similarly, courts of appeals have held that the *Feres* doctrine bars recovery by children born with birth defects that resulted from genetic changes in their fathers that occurred when they were exposed to radiation while on military duty.[34] However, "the *Feres* doctrine does not bar an action against the United States for a service-related injury suffered by a veteran as a result of independent post-service negligence," such as failure of the government to warn or monitor a veteran who had been exposed to radiation.[35] A district court has held that the *Feres* doctrine does *not* bar suit by the daughter and grandson of a soldier who was the victim of such negligence.[36]

Civilians have also been denied recovery against the United States for injuries caused by atomic testing — denied it on the basis of the discretionary function exception to the FTCA. (This exception applies to all plaintiffs, so even if the *Feres* doctrine were overturned, military personnel would be barred from recovering to the same extent as civilians in atomic testing cases.) The Supreme Court has not considered the applicability of the discretionary function exception to atomic testing cases, but it has declined to review two federal courts of appeals decisions that held that the discretionary function exception bars recovery in such cases.

In *In re Consolidated United States Atmospheric Testing Litigation*, 820 F.2d 982, 993 (9th Cir. 1987), *cert. denied*, 485 U.S. 905 (1988), the court of appeals stated that "*Dalehite* is squarely on point." In both *In re Consolidated* and

Dalehite, "a detailed and extensive Operation Plan was adopted on orders from the highest levels of the Executive Department. An integral part of that Plan was an extensive Safety Plan ... ." *Id.* at 994. The plaintiffs in *In re Consolidated* argued that the negligent failure of Atomic Energy Commission and military officials to follow safety guidelines established in the plan, such as decontamination measures and the use of protective clothing and gear, had resulted in the overexposure of many hundreds or thousands of test participants. The Ninth Circuit held:

> The Safety Plan incorporated into the Operation Plan contemplated that judgments and decisions concerning exposure to radiological hazards and the degree of protection to be afforded would be made in light of the objectives and the needs of the test program. Safety decisions, therefore, were part of the policy decisions made in the conduct of the weapons tests, [ ] and they fall squarely within the articulation in *Dalehite* that
>
> [w]here there is room for policy judgment and decision there is discretion.

Id. at 995, citing 346 U.S. at 36.

The plaintiffs also argued that the government had been negligent in failing to warn the plaintiffs "of the dangers to which they had been exposed or to monitor test participants for health problems resulting from radiation exposure." 820 F.2d at 996. The court held:

> This is not a case of failing to warn river users of hidden obstructions beneath the surface; or park users of the risk of flash floods; or a treating physician of his patient's dangerous propensities. The kind of "warning" that these [atomic testing] cases involve ... entailed a commitment of substantial resources, including the assignment of a large number of employees and the expenditure of large sums of money ... . The program required difficult judgments balancing the magnitude of the risk from radiation exposure — of which there was only fragmentary knowledge — against the risks and burdens of a public program. Those risks included the potential consequences of creating public anxiety and the health hazards inherent in the medical responses to the warning.
>
> Thus, any decision whether to issue warnings to thousands of test participants ... calls for the exercise of judgment and discretion at the highest levels of government ... .
>
> The conclusion is inescapable that every aspect of a warning program is a matter that falls within the discretionary function exception as defined in *Dalehite* and *Varig* ... .[37]

In *Allen v. United States*, 816 F.2d 1417 (10th Cir. 1987), *cert. denied*, 484 U.S. 1004 (1988), the Tenth Circuit, two months earlier, had reached the same conclusion as the Ninth Circuit reached in *In re Consolidated.* The plaintiffs in *Allen* "singled out the alleged failure of the government ... to fully monitor offsite fallout exposure and to fully provide needed public information on radioactive fallout." 816 F.2d at 1419. They contended that these activities did not involve "the kind of policy judgments protected by" the discretionary function exception. 816 F.2d at 1421. The court disagreed:

> In the case before us, as in *Varig*, the government actors had a general statutory duty to promote safety; this duty was broad and discretionary. In the case before us it was left to the AEC, as in *Varig* it was left to the Secretary of Transportation and the FAA, to decide exactly *how* to protect public safety ... . In the instant case, no evidence was presented of any act or omission of the AEC or its employees that clearly contravened a specific statutory or regulatory authority. There was no evidence, for example that the Test Information Officer failed to give out, or that the Radsafe Officer failed to take a specific radiation measurement that had been decided upon. Plaintiffs' entire case rests on the fact that the government *could* have made better plans. This is probably correct, but it is insufficient for FTCA liability.

Id. at 1421, 1424.

The Warner Amendment and the Radiation Exposure Compensation Act

Military and civilian victims of atomic testing have also sought to sue the government contractors involved in the testing. Under state tort law, a company engaged in atomic testing would likely be subject to strict liability (liability even in the absence of negligence) for injuries resulting from such testing, as atomic testing is an "abnormally dangerous" activity.[38] Federal law, however, bars victims of atomic testing from suing federal government contractors. Section 1631 of P.L. 98- 525, 42 U.S.C. § 2212 (known as the "Warner Amendment"),[39] provides that an action against the United States under the FTCA shall be the exclusive remedy for injuries "due to exposure to radiation based on acts or omissions by a contractor in carrying out an atomic weapons testing program under a contract with the United States." Under this provision, a contractor's employees shall be considered federal employees for purposes of any lawsuit.[40]

Thus, the Warner Amendment makes suits against the United States under the FTCA the exclusive remedy for claims based on atomic testing injuries. This remedy, however, is illusory, because the *Feres* doctrine precludes recovery by military personnel and the discretionary function exception precludes recovery by anyone.[41] The constitutionality of the Warner Amendment has been upheld by two federal courts of appeals.[42] Repeal of the Warner Amendment, it should be noted, would not necessarily result in liability on the part of contractors; there would still be the possibility that they could raise the government contractor defense. (On the government contractor defense, see the final section of this chapter.)

In 1990, Congress enacted the Radiation Exposure Compensation Act, 42 U.S.C. § 2210 note, a compensation program for victims of atomic testing and uranium mining. It authorizes $50,000 to be paid to any person who contracted leukemia or certain listed cancers and was physically present in an area affected by atmospheric nuclear tests for specified periods from 1951 through 1962. It also authorizes $75,000 to be paid to any person who contracted leukemia or certain listed cancers after having participated onsite in an atmospheric nuclear test. Finally, it provides $100,000 to any person employed in a uranium mine at any time from 1947 to 1971 who contracted lung cancer or a nonmalignant respiratory disease, if he was exposed to specified levels of radiation. (In none of these cases is a claimant required to prove that radiation exposure actually caused his disease.) A person who accepts compensation under the act forfeits all right to sue the United States or any federal contractor for claims arising out of the same radiation exposure. "This act was patterned in part on the Radiation-Exposed Veterans Compensation Act of 1988 (P.L. 100-321)."[43] Department of Justice regulations under the Radiation Exposure Compensation Act appear at 28 C.F.R. Part 79.

The Intentional Tort Exception

The intentional tort exception, 28 U.S.C. § 2680(h), provides that the FTCA does not apply to claims:

> arising out of assault, battery, false imprisonment, false arrest, malicious prosecution, abuse of process, libel, slander, misrepresentation, deceit, or interference with contract rights.

However, the United States may be held liable for any of the first six torts in this list if committed by an "investigative or law enforcement officer of the United States Government." 28 U.S.C. § 2680(h).[44] This exception to the intentional tort exception was enacted in 1974 and "grew out of widespread publicity given to several incidents in which federal narcotics agents engaged in what a Senate Committee described as 'abusive, illegal and unconstitutional "no-knock raids."'"[45]

In *Sheridan v. United States*, 487 U.S. 392 (1988), three naval corpsmen found a naval enlisted man named Carr unconscious from alcohol consumption and attempted to take him to a hospital emergency room. Before they reached the emergency room, Carr regained consciousness, broke away from the corpsmen, and displayed the barrel of his rifle to them. The corpsmen fled and did not alert any authority that Carr was inebriated and armed. Carr ended up near a public street and began shooting at passing vehicles, hitting one of the plaintiffs.

Because of the intentional tort exception, the plaintiffs in *Sheridan* could not sue the government based on Carr' s shooting. Therefore, they sued the government based on the three corpsmen's negligence in failing to alert authorities as to the threat posed by Carr. The government argued that the intentional tort exception barred this claim because, even though it was based on negligence, it was a claim "arising out" of assault or battery within the meaning of 28 U.S.C. § 2680(h). The Supreme Court did not rule on the government's argument because it decided for the plaintiff on another ground: that the intentional tort exception should "be construed to apply only to claims that would otherwise be authorized by the basic waiver of sovereign immunity ... . The tortious conduct of an off-duty serviceman, not acting within the scope of his office or employment, does not itself give rise to Government liability, whether that conduct is intentional or merely negligent." *Id.* at 400-401. This is because the FTCA makes the government liable only for torts committed by an employee while acting "within the scope of his office or employment." 28 U.S.C. § 1346(b). Thus, since the government could not be liable for Carr' s acts, the intentional tort exception did not apply to bar a suit based on the negligence of others that led to Carr' s acts, even if, as the government argued, the suit arose out of Carr' s intentional tort. Had Carr not been a federal employee at all, the result would have been the same: since the government could not be liable for Carr' s acts, whether such acts were negligent or intentional, the intentional tort exception would not apply to bar a suit based on the negligence of federal employees that led to Carr' s intentional tort.

The Court left open the question whether a suit based on the "negligent hiring, negligent supervision, or negligent training may ever provide the basis for liability under the FTCA for a foreseeable assault or battery by a Government employee [acting within the scope of his employment]." *Id.* at 403 n.8. On this question, there was subsequently a split in the federal circuits. *See*, *Billingsley v. United States*, 251 F.3d 696, 698 (8th Cir. 2001).

Justice Kennedy concurred in the judgment, but expressed the fear "that many, if not all, intentional torts of Government employees plausibly could be ascribed to the negligence of the tortfeasor' s supervisors." *Id.* at 407.

SUITS AGAINST FEDERAL EMPLOYEES

The Federal Employees Liability Reform and Tort Compensation Act of 1988, P.L. 100-694 (commonly know as the Westfall Act, after the Supreme Court case it overturned), amended the FTCA to make it the exclusive remedy for torts committed by federal employees within the scope of their employment.[46] In other words, it precludes federal employees from being sued for torts committed within the scope of their employment. 28 U.S.C. § 2679(b)(1).

The Westfall Act, however, provides immunity only from liability under state tort law; a federal employee may still be sued for violating the Constitution or violating a federal statute that authorizes suit against an individual. 28 U.S.C. § 2679(b)(2). Such cases are barred, however, if the claimant sues the United States under the FTCA and a judgment in the FTCA case is handed down before a judgment in the case against the employee is handed down.[47] 28 U.S.C. § 2676.[48]

In *United States v. Smith*, 499 U.S. 160 (1991), the Supreme Court held that the Westfall Act made federal employees immune from suit under state tort law even when an FTCA exception precludes recovery against the United States. In this case, the United States was immune because the claim had arisen in a foreign country.[49]

Certification

If a federal employee is sued under state tort law, in federal or state court, for conduct that may have occurred within the scope of his employment, then he may turn over papers that were served on him to the Attorney General, and the Attorney General may certify that the federal employee "was acting within the scope of employment at the time of the incident out of which the claim arose."[50] If the Attorney General makes this certification, the United States is substituted for the employee as a defendant in the action.[51] The Attorney General's certification conclusively establishes that the defendant had been acting within the "scope of office or employment for purposes of remov[ing]" a case from state court to federal district court.[52] If the Attorney General refuses to certify that the federal employee "was acting within scope of employment," then the employee may petition the court in which he was sued for certification that he had been acting within the scope of employment.[53] If the court certifies that he had been acting within the scope of employment, then the United States will be substituted as a defendant.[54] If the court that made this certification was a state court, then the Attorney General may remove the case to a federal district court, but if the federal district court finds that the employee's actions were not within the scope of employment, then the case must be remanded to state court.[55]

The Supreme Court has decided two cases addressing the certification provisions. In *Gutierrez de Martinez v. Lamagno*, 515 U.S. 417 (1995), the Supreme Court held that the Attorney General's certification that a federal employee acted within the scope of employment is reviewable in court. The majority opinion explained:

> When a federal employee is sued for a wrongful or negligent act, the [Westfall Act] empowers the Attorney General to certify that the employee "was acting within the scope of his office or employment at the time of the incident out of which the claim arose ... ." 28 U.S.C. § 2679(d)(1). Upon certification, the employee is dismissed from the action and the United States is substituted as defendant. The case then falls under the governance of the [FTCA] ... . If, however, an exception to the FTCA shields the United States from suit, the party may be left without a tort action against any party.

Id. at 4 19-420. This is what occurred in this case, so, "[e]ndeavoring to redeem their lawsuit, plaintiffs ... sought review of the Attorney General's scope-of-employment certification, for if the employee was acting outside the scope of his employment, the plaintiffs' tort action could proceed against him. The lower court held the certification unreviewable." *Id.* at 420. The Supreme Court reversed, finding that "Congress did not address this precise issue unambiguously, if at all," and "that judicial review of executive action 'will not be cut off unless there is persuasive reason to believe that such was the purpose of Congress.'" *Id.* at 424.[56]

In *Osborn v. Haley*, 127 S. Ct. 881 (2007), a federal employee had been sued in state court, and the Attorney General had certified that the employee had been acting within the scope of employment. The federal district court had invalidated the Attorney General's certification, finding it improper because the government maintained that the incident in dispute never happened. The federal district court then remanded the suit to the state court, thereby preventing the United States from substituting itself as a defendant. The court of appeals vacated the district court decision and the Supreme Court affirmed the court of appeals decision. The

Supreme Court held that the Attorney General's certification was proper and that the United States must remain as a substitute defendant "unless and until the District Court determines that the employee, *in fact* ... engaged in conduct beyond the scope of his employment." 127 S. Ct. at 888. Next, the Supreme Court examined two conflicting statutory provisions to determine whether a case that the Attorney General had certified and that had been removed from a state court to a federal district court could be remanded to the state court. One provision, 28 U.S.C. § 2679(d)(2), states that the Attorney General's certification is conclusive for the purposes of removing a case from a state court to a federal district court. The other provision, 28 U.S.C. § 1447(d), bars appellate review of "[a]n order remanding a case to the State court from which it was removed." The Supreme Court held that 28 U.S.C. § 2679(d)(2) controls, so that once an Attorney General certifies, requiring the action to be removed from state court to federal district court, the federal district court must retain jurisdiction and cannot remand.

Constitutional Torts: Federal Employees' Liability and Immunity

Although the FTCA does not immunize federal employees when they violate the Constitution, common law sometimes does. Before examining federal employees' immunity from liability for constitutional torts, however, it is necessary to discuss their liability for such torts.[57] In *Bivens v. Six Unknown Named Agents*, 403 U.S. 388 (1971), federal agents, without a warrant, entered and searched the plaintiff's apartment and arrested the plaintiff for alleged narcotics violations. A state official who commits such a tort, in addition to being subject to liability under state tort law, may be sued under 42 U.S.C. § 1983, which provides that any person who, under color of any state statute, deprives another person of rights secured by the Constitution or a federal statute, shall be liable to the person injured. A federal official who commits a constitutional tort is not subject to liability under state tort law (because of the Westfall Act), and no statute similar to § 1983 makes federal officials liable under federal law for violating another person's constitutional rights. In *Bivens* and subsequent cases, however, the Supreme Court held that such a statute is not necessary for an injured party to recover damages from a federal official who commits a constitutional tort.[58] "Having concluded that petitioner's complaint states a cause of action under the Fourth Amendment, *supra*, at 390-395, we hold that petitioner is entitled to recover money damages for any injuries he has suffered as a result of the agents' violation of the Amendment." *Id.* at 397.[59]

Subsequently, however, the Supreme Court indicated "that such a remedy may not be available when 'special factors counselling hesitation' are present." *Chappell v. Wallace*, 462 U.S. 296, 298 (1983). In *Chappell*, five Navy enlisted men charged their superior officers with treating them differently because of their minority race. Guided by "the Court's analysis in *Feres*" (*id.* at 299), the Supreme Court in *Chappell* held:

> Taken together, the unique disciplinary structure of the Military Establishment and Congress' activity in the field constitute "special factors" which dictate that it would be inappropriate to provide enlisted military personnel a *Bivens*-type remedy against their superior officers.

Id. at 304.[60]

In *United States v. Stanley*, 483 U.S. 669 (1987), the Army had given a serviceman LSD without his knowledge, which caused him to suffer severe personality changes that led to his discharge and the dissolution of his marriage. The Supreme Court indicated that *Feres* barred his claim against the government, and that *Chappell* barred his claim against the officers involved. The plaintiff had sought to distinguish his case from *Chappell* on the grounds that, unlike in *Chappell*,

> the defendants in this case were not Stanley's superior military officers, and indeed may well have been civilian personnel, and that the chain-of-command concerns at the heart of *Chappell* ... are thus not implicated. Second, Stanley argues that there is no evidence that this injury was "incident to service."

Id. at 679-680. The Court found that the second argument was not available to Stanley because the issue of service incidence had been decided adversely to him previously.

> As for his first argument, Stanley and the lower courts may well be correct that *Chappell* implicated military chain-of command concerns more directly than do the facts alleged here ... . It is therefore true that *Chappell* is not strictly controlling, in the sense that no holding can be broader than the facts before the court.

Id. at 680. However, the Court added:

> Since *Feres* did not consider the officer-subordinate relationship crucial, but established instead an "incident to service" test, it is plain that our reasoning in

> *Chappell* does not support the distinction Stanley would rely on ... . Today, no more than when we wrote *Chappell*, do we see any reason why our judgment in the *Bivens* context should be any less protective of military concerns than it has been with respect to FTCA suits, where we adopted an "incident to service" rule.

Id. at 680-681. Thus, with respect to injuries incurred incident to service as a result of constitutional torts, the principle behind the *Feres* doctrine applies equally to preclude military personnel from suing either the government under the FTCA or federal officials under *Bivens*.[61]

In addition to situations with "special factors counselling hesitation," *Bivens*-type actions are not permitted "when defendants show that Congress has provided an alternative remedy which it explicitly declared to be a *substitute* for recovery directly under the Constitution and viewed as equally effective." *Carlson v. Green*, 446 U.S. 14, 18-19 (1980) (emphasis in original).[62] The Court in *Carlson v. Green* allowed a *Bivens*-type action against a federal prison official for violating the Cruel and Unusual Punishment Clause of the Eighth Amendment. The defendant argued that Congress had intended a suit against the United States under the FTCA as an alternative remedy, but the Court held:

> When Congress amended the FTCA in 1974 to create a cause of action against the United States for intentional torts committed by federal law enforcement officers, 28 U.S.C. § 2680(h), the congressional comments accompanying that amendment made it crystal clear that Congress views FTCA and *Bivens* as parallel, complementary causes of action.[63]

Id. at 20.

In subsequent cases, the Supreme Court has continued to limit the availability of *Bivens* actions. In *FDIC v. Meyer*, 510 U.S. 471 (1994), the Court declined "to extend *Bivens* to permit suit against a federal agency, even though the agency — because Congress had waived sovereign immunity — was otherwise amenable to suit."[64] In *Correctional Services Corporation v. Malesko*, 534 U.S. 61 (2001), the Court held that *Bivens* actions may not be brought "against private entities acting under color of federal law" (*id.* at 66) — in this case "against a private corporation operating a halfway house under contract with the Bureau of Prisons" (*id.* at 63). Explaining its decisions in both *Meyer* and *Malesko*, the Court in *Malesko* said that the purpose of *Bivens* is to deter individual officers, not policymaking entities, from committing unconstitutional acts. Does this mean that an individual officer of a private entity acting under color of federal law would be subject to a *Bivens* action? The Court in *Malesko* did not decide the question.

In *Wilkie v. Robbins*, 127 S. Ct. 2588, 2598 (2007), the Supreme Court explained that

> the decision whether to recognize a *Bivens* remedy may require two steps. In the first place, there is the question whether any alternative, existing process for protecting [a constitutionally recognized] interest amounts to a convincing reason for the Judicial Branch to refrain from providing a new and freestanding remedy in damages. But even in the absence of an alternative, a *Bivens* remedy is a subject of judgment: "the federal courts must make the kind of remedial determination that is appropriate for a common-law tribunal, paying special heed, however, to any special factors counseling hesitation before authorizing a new kind of federal litigation." [Citations omitted.]

In *Wilkie v. Robbins*, the plaintiff had sought damages from officials of the Bureau of Land Management, whom he "accused of harassment and intimidation aimed at extracting an easement across private property." *Id.* at 2593. The Court, applying the two steps it cited, declined to allow a *Bivens* action, finding that "[a] judicial standard to identify illegitimate pressure going beyond legitimately hard bargaining would be endlessly knotty to work out ... and would invite an onslaught of *Bivens* actions." *Id.* at 2604.

The Practical Side of *Bivens* Actions

According to one commentator, "[i]ndividual liability under *Bivens* is fictional ... because the federal government in practice functions as the real party in interest, paying for representation and reimbursing the sued individuals when they settle or pay judgments."[65]

"*Bivens* has, however," the commentator continues,

> proved to be a surreptitiously progovernment decision. Although it appears to provide a mechanism for remedying constitutional violations, its application has rarely led to damages recoveries. Government figures reflect that, out of approximately 12,000 *Bivens* claims filed between 1971 and 1985, *Bivens* plaintiffs actually obtained a judgment that was not reversed on appeal in only four cases. While similar figures have not been systematically kept since 1985, recoveries from both settlements and litigated judgments continue to be extraordinarily rare. According to one estimate, plaintiffs obtain a judgment awarding them damages in a fraction of one percent of *Bivens* cases and obtain a monetary settlement in less than one percent of such cases.[66]

Qualified Immunity to *Bivens* Actions

Having summarized the law governing federal employees' liability for constitutional torts, we return to the question of their common law immunity from liability for such torts. (The FTCA, it will be recalled, gives them immunity only from state tort law.) Such immunity is generally qualified, yet "[q]ualified immunity is undoubtedly the most significant bar to constitutional tort actions."[67] In *Butz v. Economou,* 438 U.S. 478, 507 (1978), the Supreme Court held

> that, in a suit for damages arising from unconstitutional action, federal executive officials exercising discretion are entitled only to the qualified immunity specified in *Scheuer*, subject to those exceptional situations where it is demonstrated that absolute immunity is essential for the conduct of public business.

In *Scheuer v. Rhodes*, 416 U.S. 232, 247-248 (1974), referred to in this quotation, the Supreme Court held that state executive officers are immune from liability under 42 U.S.C. § 1983

> in varying scope, ... the variation being dependent upon the scope of discretion and responsibilities of the office and all the circumstances as they reasonably appeared at the time of the action on which liability is sought to be based. It is the existence of reasonable grounds for the belief formed at the time and in light of the circumstances, coupled with good-faith belief, that affords a basis for qualified immunity of executive officers for acts performed in the course of official conduct.

Because, under *Butz*, the *Scheuer* standard applies to federal as well as to state officials, if a federal official, in the exercise of a discretionary function, violates a person's constitutional rights, he may be subject to liability, even though the discretionary function exception of the FTCA would preclude liability on the part of the government.[68] Congress, however, has the power to grant additional immunity to federal officials. *See*, *Butz*, 438 U.S. at 500.

The Government Contractor Defense

In *Boyle v. United Technologies Corp.*, 487 U.S. 500, 504 (1988), the Supreme Court held that "uniquely federal interests" in the government's procurement of equipment require that a "government contractor defense" be available in certain cases. This is a defense that manufacturers may assert in products liability cases alleging design defects. These are cases, brought under state law, in which the plaintiff alleges that his injuries were caused by a product that was defective in that the manufacturer failed to use the safest feasible design for the product. In its defense, the manufacturer may assert that it manufactured the product pursuant to a government contract and that the design it used was required by contract specifications. In *Boyle*, the Supreme Court held that, notwithstanding state law, "federal common law" requires that the government contractor defense be available in certain cases.[69] This is because "[t]he imposition of liability on Government contractors will directly affect the terms of Government contracts: either the contractor will decline to manufacture the design specified by the Government, or it will raise its price. Either way, the interests of the United States will be directly affected." *Id.* at 507.

The Court found that displacement of state law will occur only where "a 'significant conflict' exists between an identifiable 'federal policy or interest and the [operation] of state law,' ... or the application of state law would 'frustrate specific objectives' of federal legislation ... ." *Id.* A significant conflict may exist, the Court found, where "the state-imposed duty of care that is the asserted basis of the contractor's liability ... is precisely contrary to the duty imposed by the Government contract." *Id.* at 509. In some cases, however, the state-imposed duty of care will not conflict with the federal contract, or, even if it does, will not be significant, as where "a federal procurement officer orders, by model number, a quantity of stock [items that happen to have a design defect]." *Id.* In such cases, the government contractor defense would not be available.

Boyle was a suit by the father of a Marine who had been killed incident to service in a helicopter accident, allegedly caused by the helicopter's having been defectively designed. The lower court had allowed the government contractor defense on the basis of the reasoning behind the *Feres* doctrine. As the Supreme Court explained: "Military contractor liability would conflict with this doctrine, the Fourth Circuit reasoned, since the increased cost of the contractor's tort liability would be added to the price of the contract, and '[s]uch pass-through costs would ... defeat the purpose of the immunity for military accidents conferred upon the government itself.'" *Id.* at 510.[70] The Supreme Court did not adopt the *Feres* doctrine as the basis for the government contractor defense:

> Since that doctrine covers only service-related injuries, and not injuries caused by the military to civilians, it could not be invoked to prevent, for example, a civilian's suit against the manufacturer of fighter planes, based on a state tort theory, claiming harm from what is alleged to be needlessly high levels

> of noise produced by jet engines. Yet we think that the character of the jet engines the Government orders for its fighter planes cannot be regulated by state tort law, no more in suits by civilians than in suits by members of the Armed Services.

Id. at 510-511. Rather, the Court found that the reasoning behind the discretionary function exception furnished a better basis for the government contractor defense:

> We think that the selection of the appropriate design for military equipment to be used by our Armed Forces is assuredly a discretionary function within the meaning of this provision ... . The financial burden of judgments against the contractors would ultimately be passed through, substantially if not totally, to the United States itself, since defense contractors will predictably raise their prices to cover, or to insure against, contingent liability for the Government-ordered designs ... . In sum, we are of the view that state law which holds Government contractors liable for design defects in military equipment does in some circumstances present a "significant conflict" with federal policy and must be displaced.

Id. at 511-512. Delineating these circumstances, the Court ruled:

> Liability for design defects in military equipment cannot be imposed, pursuant to state law, when (1) the United States approved reasonably precise specifications; (2) the equipment conformed to those specifications; and (3) the supplier warned the United States about the dangers in the use of the equipment that were known to the supplier but not to the United States. The first two of these conditions assure that the suit is within the area where the policy of the "discretionary function" would be frustrated — *i.e.*, they assure that the design feature in question was considered by a Government officer, and not merely by the contractor itself. The third condition is necessary because, in its absence, the displacement of state tort law would create some incentive for the manufacturer to withhold knowledge of risks ... [thereby] cutting off information highly relevant to the discretionary decision.

Id. at 512.

Although the defendant in *Boyle* was a military contractor, and the Court throughout its opinion refers to military equipment, the fact that it based its opinion on the discretionary function exception and not on the *Feres* doctrine seems to indicate that the government contractor defense is available to both civilian and military contractors. In *Nielson v. George Diamond Vogel Paint Co.*, 892 F.2d 1450 (9th Cir. 1990), the court acknowledged that the Supreme Court's reliance on the discretionary function exception meant that the government contractor defense can in principle apply to civilian equipment. "Yet," it added, "the policy behind the defense remains rooted in considerations peculiar to the military." *Id.* at 1455. In the case before it, which involved civilian equipment, it found "no reason to hold that the application of state law would create a 'significant conflict' with federal policy requiring a displacement of state law." *Id.* There is currently a split in the circuits over the applicability of the government contractor defense to non-military contractors.[71]

In *Hercules, Inc. v. United States*, 516 U.S. 417 (1996), the Supreme Court rejected a claim by Agent Orange manufacturers that they were entitled to reimbursement from the government for the costs of defending and settling tort claims brought against them by Vietnam veterans who were injured by the chemical. The government had "prescribed the formula and detailed specifications for manufacture" (*id.* at 419), but the settlement with the veterans occurred before *Boyle* established the government contractor defense.

The manufacturers sued the United States under the Tucker Act, 28 U.S.C. §§ 1346(a), 149 1(a), which authorizes suits against the United States founded upon "any express or implied contract." They alleged an implied agreement by the government to reimburse them for tort liability, and a breach of the contractual warranty of specifications. As to the first, the Court held that there was no contract either express or implied in fact; as to the second, the Court held that the government "warrants that the contractor will be able to perform the contract satisfactorily if it follows the specifications" (*id.* at 425), but that this warranty does not extend to third-party claims against the contractor.

ENDNOTES

[1] Federal Housing Administration v. Burr, 309 U.S. 242, 244 (1940).

[2] United States v. Chemical Foundation, Inc., 272 U.S. 1, 20 (1926).

[3] The United States may be held liable under the FTCA for torts of employees of the executive, legislative, and judicial branches, but not for torts of government contractors. 28 U.S.C. § 2671.

[4] Another section of the FTCA provides that the United States shall be liable "in the same manner and to the same extent as a private individual under like circumstances" (28 U.S.C. § 2674(a)), and the Supreme Court has noted that

"like circumstances" are not limited to "the same circumstances," but include "analogous" circumstances. United States v. Olson, 546 U.S. 43, 47 (2005).

[5] United States v. Olson, *supra*, note 4.

[6] Federal civilian employees covered by the Federal Employees' Compensation Act, 5 U.S.C. §§ 8101 *et seq.*, are also prohibited from suing under the FTCA for work-related injuries. 5 U.S.C. § 8116(c).

[7] The requirement in 28 U.S.C. § 1346(b) that liability be based on a "negligent or wrongful act or omission" has been construed to preclude strict liability. *See*, Dalehite v. United States, 346 U.S. 15, 44-45 (1953). However, the National Swine Flu Immunization Program of 1976, P.L. 94-380, made the United States liable for injuries arising out of the administration of the swine flu vaccine to the extent that manufacturers would be liable under state law "including negligence, strict liability in tort, and breach of warranty."

[8] In *Molzof v. United States*, 502 U.S. 301 (1992), the Supreme Court held that damages for future medical expenses and loss of enjoyment of life for a veteran in a permanent vegetative state as a result of government hospital employees' negligence were not "punitive" and therefore could be awarded. The government had argued that these damages were punitive rather than compensatory in nature because the award for future medical expenses duplicated free medical services already being provided by the veterans' hospital, and the award for loss of enjoyment of life cannot redress a comatose patient's uncognizable loss. The Court held, however, "that § 2674 bars the recovery only of what are legally considered 'punitive damages' under traditional common-law principles." *Id.* at 312 (emphasis in original).

[9] Subsequent exceptions cited in the sentence also appear in 28 U.S.C. § 2680.

[10] In *Dolan v. United States Postal Service*, 546 U.S. 481 (2006), the Supreme Court held that the postal exception is inapplicable to a claim that mail left on the plaintiff's porch caused her to trip and fall, just as it is inapplicable to the negligent operation of postal motor vehicles. "Congress intended to retain immunity," the Court wrote, "only for injuries arising, directly or consequentially, because mail either fails to arrive at all or arrives late, in damaged condition, or at the wrong address." *Id.* at 489. Losses of this type, the Court added, "are at least to some degree avoidable or compensable through postal registration and insurance." *Id.* at 490.

[11] Section 6241 of the Technical and Miscellaneous Revenue Act of 1988, P.L. 100-647, authorizes taxpayers to sue the United States if "any officer or employee of the Internal Revenue Service recklessly or intentionally disregards" any provision of the Internal Revenue Code, and to recover up to

$100,000 in "actual, direct economic damages" sustained as a result of such action. 26 U.S.C. § 7433.

[12] Public Law 106-185 (2000) added an exception to this exception to the FTCA, allowing suits in some cases involving forfeiture of property other than as a sentence for a crime. In *Ali v. Federal Bureau of Prisons*, 128 S. Ct. 831, 834 (2008), the Court held "that the broad phrase 'any other law enforcement officer' covers all law enforcement officers," including officers of the Federal Bureau of Prisons, and does not apply "only to law enforcement [12] officers enforcing customs or excise laws."

[13] In *Smith v. United States*, 507 U.S. 197, 198 (1993), the Supreme Court held that Antarctica is a foreign country for this purpose even though it is "a sovereignless region without civil tort law of its own." In *Sosa v. Alvarez-Machain*, 542 U.S. 692, 712 (2004), the Supreme Court held "that the FTCA's foreign country exception bars all claims based on any injury suffered in a foreign country, regardless of where the tortious act or omission occurred." The plaintiff's suit therefore was dismissed even though his "abduction in Mexico was the direct result of wrongful acts of planning and direction by DEA agents located in California." *Id.* at 702. The Court was unwilling to adopt the "headquarters doctrine" because "it will virtually always be possible to assert that the negligent activity that injured the plaintiff [abroad] was the consequence of faulty training, selection or supervision — or even less than that, lack of careful training, selection or supervision — in the United States." *Id.*

Although the United States is not liable for claims arising in a foreign country, federal statutes give several federal agencies the authority to compensate victims of torts committed by federal employees in foreign countries. These statutes include 22 U.S.C. §§ 1475(5), 2269(f), 2269-1 (Department of State), 38 U.S.C. § 5 15(b) (Department of Veterans Affairs), 22 U.S.C. § 2509(b) (Peace Corps), and 10 U.S.C. §§ 2733, 2734 (Department of Defense).

[14] In *McNeil v. United States*, 508 U.S. 106 (1993), the Supreme Court disallowed a suit because the claimant had not first filed an administrative claim, even though the claimant was a prisoner without legal counsel and had filed an administrative claim (later denied) only four months after filing suit, before any substantial progress in the litigation had occurred.

[15] A claim accrues under the FTCA when "the plaintiff has discovered both his injury and its cause." United States v. Kubrick, 444 U.S. 111, 120 (1979). This rule benefits, among others, plaintiffs with latent diseases that are not discovered until years after exposure to a hazardous substance. *See also*,

Sinclair and Szypszak, *Limitations of Action Under the FTCA: A Synthesis and Proposal*, 28 Harvard Journal on Legislation 1 (1991); Annotation, *Statute of Limitations Under Federal Tort Claims Act (28 USCS § 2401(b))*, 29 ALR Fed 482.

[16] Pascale v. United States, 998 F.2d 186 (3d Cir. 1993).

[17] *See*, Kirst, *Jury Trial and the Federal Tort Claims Act: Time to Recognize the Seventh Amendment Right*, 58 Texas Law Review 549 (1980).

[18] 28 U.S.C. § 2672, as amended by P.L. 10 1-552, § 8; 38 U.S.C. § 515. There appears to be no general limit on settlements effected with the prior written approval of the Attorney General or his designee. A limit applicable to the Department of Justice in non-FTCA situations is noted in footnote 45 of this report.

[19] 28 U.S.C. § 2672, as amended by P.L. 10 1-552, § 8; *see also*, 38 U.S.C. § 515.

[20] 28 C.F.R. § 0.168(d)(2); *see*, Lester Jayson and Robert Longstreth, HANDLING FEDERAL TORT CLAIMS: ADMINISTRATIVE AND JUDICIAL REMEDIES, § 15.05[1]. The Attorney General has delegated the authority to settle tort claims of up to $200,000 to the Secretary of Veterans Affairs, the Postmaster General, the Secretary of Defense, and the Secretary of Health and Human Services, and of up to $100,000 to the Secretary of Transportation. 28 C.F.R. Part 14, App.

[21] *See*, Annotation, *Calculations of Attorneys' Fees Under Federal Tort Claims Act — 28 USCS § 2678*, 86 ALR Fed 866. A California statute that limited the amount of attorneys' fees that may be charged a client in a medical malpractice action was held to be preempted to the extent that it would apply in an action brought under the FTCA. Jackson v. United States, 881 F.2d 707 (9th Cir. 1989).

[22] The pertinent part of this provision, which is part of the Equal Access to Justice Act, states: "The United States shall be liable for such fees [i.e., reasonable attorneys' fees] and expenses to the same extent that any other party would be liable under the common law or under the terms of any statute which specifically provides for such an award." No statute provides for fee awards under FTCA, and another part of the Equal Access to Justice Act, which authorizes fee awards against the United States in some instances where other parties would not be liable for fee awards, does not apply to "cases sounding in tort." 28 U.S.C. § 24 12(d)(1)(A). However, under the common law, parties other than the United States may be held liable for attorneys' fees when they act in bad faith. Alyeska Pipeline Service Co. v. Wilderness Society, 421 U.S. 240, 258-259 (1975).

In *Sanchez v. Rowe*, 870 F.2d 291, 295 (5th Cir. 1989), the court found a lack of the requisite bad faith and therefore did "not reach the issue whether an award of attorneys fees would ... be barred by the FTCA prohibition against punitive damages [28 U.S.C. § 2674]." Subsequently, however, in *Molzof v. United States*, *supra*, note 8, the Supreme Court, in a different context, held "that § 2674 bars the recovery only of what are legally considered 'punitive damages' under traditional common-law principles."

23 804 F.2d 561 (9th Cir. 1986), *modified*, 813 F.2d 1006 (9th Cir. 1987), *withdrawn*, 825 F.2d 202 (9th Cir. 1987), *cert. denied*, 485 U.S. 987 (1988).

24 The three original reasons Justice Scalia referred to were that "the parallel private liability required by the FTCA was absent" and the first two reasons mentioned in *Stencel*; the "military discipline" rationale was the third reason mentioned in *Stencel.*

25 The three rationales referred to are those cited in *Stencel* and by the majority in *Johnson*.

26 833 F.2d at 286 (citing *Shearer*, 473 U.S. at 56, and adding emphasis).

27 *See*, e.g., *Medical Malpractice Suits for Armed Services Personnel: Hearings on S. 2490 and H.R. 1054 Before the Subcomm. on Courts and Administrative Practice of the Senate Comm. on the Judiciary*, 100th Cong., 2nd sess. (1988).

28 Congress has provided that the discretionary function exception does not apply in any action based upon the act or omission of a participant in the swine flu immunization program. P.L. 94-380; *see also*, note 7, *supra*. Congress has also provided that the exception does not apply to certain claims based upon gross negligence by employees of the Consumer Product Safety Commission. 15 U.S.C. § 2053(h)(1)(B).

29 More generally, the Court noted:

> As in *Dalehite*, it is unnecessary — and indeed impossible — to define with precision every contour of the discretionary function exception. From the legislative and judicial materials, however, it is possible to isolate several factors useful in determining when the acts of a Government employee are protected from liability by § 268 0(a). First, it is the nature of the conduct, rather than the status of the actor, that governs whether the discretionary function exception applies in a given case ... . Second, whatever else the discretionary function exception may include, it plainly was intended to encompass the discretionary acts of the Government acting in its role as a regulator of the conduct of private individuals.

467 U.S. at 813-814.

30 More generally, the Court held that, in determining the applicability of the discretionary function exception, a court must first consider whether the

action is a matter of choice for the acting employee ... . [C]onduct cannot be discretionary unless it involves an element of judgment or choice ... . Thus, the discretionary function exception will not apply when a federal statute, regulation, or policy specifically prescribes a course of action for an employee to follow. In this event, the employee has no rightful option but to adhere to the directive ... . The [discretionary function] exception ... protects only governmental actions and decisions based on considerations of public policy.

486 U.S. at 536-537.

[31] The Court noted that some discretionary acts are not protected by the discretionary function exception because they are not "based on the purposes that the regulatory regime seeks to accomplish." If an official engaged in an act protected by the discretionary function exception drove an automobile in connection with that act and negligently caused an accident, the exception would not apply. "Although driving requires the constant exercise of discretion, the official's decisions in exercising this discretion can hardly be said to be grounded in regulatory policy." *Id.* at 325 n.7.

[32] Jayson and Longstreth, *supra*, note 20, § 5A.09 (footnotes omitted). *See*, Annotation, *Right of Member of Family of Serviceman to Maintain Action Under Federal Tort Claims Act (28 USCS §§ 1346(b), 2671 -2680) Against United States Based Upon Injuries Sustained By Serviceman While on Active Duty*, 69 ALR Fed 949.

[33] E.g., Hinkie v. United States, 715 F.2d 96 (3d Cir. 1983), *cert. denied*, 465 U.S. 1023 (1984) (barring a suit for the soldier's spouse's miscarriages and children's birth defects where these injuries were caused by chromosomal damages resulting from "the Army's negligent exposure of their husband and father to harmful levels of radiation in the course of his former military service," *id.* at 98 n.2). The court stated that it sensed the "injustice" of the result, but that it has "no legal authority, as an intermediate appellate court, to decide the case differently." *Id.* at 97.

[34] *Id.*

[35] Broudy v. United States, 722 F.2d 566, 570 (9th Cir. 1983).

[36] Seveny v. United States Government, Department of Navy, 550 F. Supp. 653 (D. R.I. 1982).

[37] *Id.* at 996-998 (quoting the district court's opinion). The court's reference to the levels of government at which decisions were made should be read in the light of the following language from the Supreme Court's decision in *Varig* (already quoted in footnote 29 of this report), which the court in *In re Consolidated* had itself quoted earlier in its opinion (820 F.2d at 995): "it is

the nature of the conduct, rather than the status of the actor, that governs whether the discretionary function exception applies in a given case."

[38] See, Prosser and Keeton, *The Law of Torts* (5th ed. 1984) § 79, p. 558.

[39] This provision was repealed and re-enacted (as the Atomic Testing Liability Act, 42 U.S.C. § 2210 note) by sections 3140 and 3141 of P.L. 101-510. This, according to the accompanying conference report, was "in order to recodify this section together with the revised Radiation Exposure Compensation Act. The conferees do not intend for this action to have any effect whatsoever on pending or past cases involving this provision of law." H.Rept. 101-923, 101st Cong., 2nd sess. 763 (1990); *reprinted in* 1990 U.S.C.C.A.N. 3270.

[40] The reason for the Warner Amendment was that the government contractors —

> provided scientific, engineering and technical support for nuclear tests carried out by the government and for the government in the exercise of a governmental function, i.e., providing for the national defense. These organizations did not order the tests to be performed; they did not set the times or places for the tests; nor did they direct military or civilian government personnel to participate in them. It should appear, without question, that these contractors were acting as the de facto instruments of the United States Government in carrying out a governmental purpose.
>
> In the litigious atmosphere that now pervades the United States, especially where atomic energy matters are concerned, literally thousands of plaintiffs have filed suits against the operators of the government laboratories that have participated in the government's nuclear weapons tests ... . Plaintiffs are seeking tens of billions of dollars in damages. Because the contractors are fully indemnified by the government under the terms of their contracts, the taxpayer will ultimately bear this burden.

S.Rept. 98-500, 98th Cong., 2nd sess. 376 (1984). Although the contractors were indemnified,

> Congress has nevertheless perceived these lawsuits to constitute a threat to the continued participation of the private contractors in the nuclear weapons program because the contractors fear the bad publicity generated by the suits.

Hammond v. United States, 786 F.2d 8, 14 (1st Cir. 1986).

[41] H.Rept. 99-567, 99th Cong., 2nd sess. 3 (1986), states that "the real effect of the Warner Amendment is to leave the harmed individuals with no remedy at all."

[42] In re Consolidated United States Atmospheric Testing Litigation, 820 F.2d 982 (9th Cir. 1987), *cert. denied*, 485 U.S. 905 (1988); Hammond v. United States, 786 F.2d 8 (1st Cir. 1986).

[43] H.Rept. 101-923, 101st Cong., 2nd sess. 762 (1990); *reprinted in* 1990 U.S.C.C.A.N. 3269.

[44] There are other exceptions to the intentional tort exception. The United States may be held liable for "misrepresentation or deceit on the part of the [Consumer Product Safety] Commission or any employee thereof ... ." 15 U.S.C. § 2053(h)(1)(A). (The CPSC is also the subject of an exception to the discretionary function exception; *see*, note 28, *supra*.) In addition, several statutes make the intentional tort exception inapplicable to causes of action arising out of negligence in the performance of medical or legal services by specified federal employees. If these statutes did not make the intentional tort exception inapplicable, then the intentional tort exception could bar recovery in malpractice actions arising out of negligence because "a particular type of claim can be viewed, under traditional concepts, as one type of tort rather than another, for example as an assault and battery rather than negligence ... . Illustrative is the case of *Moos v. United States* [225 F.2d 705 (8th Cir. 1955)] where the claimant entered a Veterans Administration hospital for an operation on his left leg and hip; the surgeons, instead, erroneously operated on his right leg and hip; the claim was held barred on the sound technical theory that the unconsented operation on the right leg and hip constituted an assault and battery and that such was the basis of the claim even though it may have been accompanied by or preceded by negligence." Jayson and Longstreth, *supra*, note 20, at § 13.06[1] [a]. *See also*, Franklin v. United States, 992 F.2d 1492, 1495 (10th Cir. 1993) ("intentional tort exclusion bars a claim for damages based on the unauthorized performance of surgery ... . [H]owever ... , the operation of that exclusion is nullified ... by an immunity statute [38 U.S.C. § 4116(f), today § 7316(f)] dealing specifically with medical tort claims arising out of the actions of Veterans Administration (VA) personnel").

The statutes that make the intentional tort exception inapplicable in these circumstances include 10 U.S.C. § 1054(e) (legal malpractice by employees of the Department of Defense); 10 U.S.C. § 1089(e) (medical malpractice by employees of the armed forces, National Guard, Department of Defense, United States Soldiers' and Airmen's Home, or Central Intelligence Agency); 22 U.S.C. § 2702(e) (medical malpractice by Department of State employees); 38 U.S.C. § 7316(f) (medical malpractice by Department of Veterans Affairs employees); 42 U.S.C. § 23 3(e) (medical malpractice by Public Health Service employees); 42 U.S.C. § 2458a(e) (medical malpractice by National Aeronautics and Space Administration employees).

[45] Jayson and Longstreth, *supra*, note 20, at § 13 .06[1] [b]. The Attorney General may settle, for not more than $50,000 in any one case, a claim for damages caused by an investigative or law enforcement officer as defined in 28 U.S.C.

§ 2680(h) who is employed by the Department of Justice acting within the scope of employment that may not be settled under the FTCA. *See* 31 U.S.C. §§ 3724 and 3724 note. *See also* note 18, *supra*. In addition, the Tariff Act of 1930 authorizes the Secretary of Homeland Security to settle claims of up to $50,000 that cannot be settled under the FTCA. 19 U.S.C. § 1630.

[46] This statute overturned *Westfall v. Erwin*, 484 U.S. 292 (1988), which held that "absolute immunity from state law tort actions should be available only when the conduct of federal officials is within the scope of their official duties *and* that conduct is discretionary in nature." *Id.* at 297-298 (emphasis in original). Prior to enactment of this statute, however, some federal employees were already immune from suit. For example, 28 U.S.C. § 2679(b), prior to its amendment by P.L. 100-694, made the FTCA the exclusive remedy for injuries "resulting from the operation by any employee of the Government of any motor vehicle while acting within the scope of his office or employment." (This was known as the Federal Drivers Act.) Other statutes made the FTCA the exclusive remedy for damages resulting from legal malpractice by employees of the Department of Defense (10 U.S .C. § 1054), and medical malpractice by employees of the Department of Veterans Affairs (38 U.S.C. § 7316 (renumbered by P.L. 102-40 from 38 U.S.C. § 4116)), the Department of State (22 U.S.C. § 2702), the Public Health Service (42 U.S.C. § 233(a)), the National Aeronautics and Space Administration (42 U.S.C. § 2458a), or the armed forces, Department of Defense, United States Soldiers' and Airmen's Home, or Central Intelligence Agency (10 U.S.C. § 1089).

[47] The case against the employee is barred whether the judgment in the FTCA case is for or against the United States. Farmer v. Perrill, 275 F.3d 958, 963 n.7 (10th Cir. 2001). If the judgment in the case against the employee is handed down first, then the plaintiff may secure judgments on both claims, but may not recover damages more than once. Turner v. Ralston, 409 F. Supp. 1260 (W.D. Wis. 1976).

[48] In *Will v. Hallock*, 546 U.S. 345 (2006), the Supreme Court held that, if a federal district court rules on a motion that § 2676 constitutes a bar against a suit against a federal employee, then 28 U.S.C. § 1291 precludes an appeal of that ruling, as the "collateral order doctrine" does not apply. By contrast, rulings that reject an employee's claim of absolute or qualified immunity are immediately appealable under the collateral order doctrine.

[49] As to the immunity for such claims, *see* text accompanying n.13, *supra*. The employee who allegedly committed the tort in this case was a military physician, and claimed immunity under the Gonzalez Act, 10 U.S.C. § 1089 (*see*, note 46, *supra*). The Ninth Circuit held that the Gonzalez Act protects

only military medical personnel who commit torts within the United States. The Supreme Court did not rule on this issue, because it found the defendant immune under P.L. 100-694. *See also*, Annotation, *Construction and Application of Westfall Act Provision Providing Federal Employee Immunity From Ordinary Tort Suits if Attorney General Certifies that Employee was Acting Within Scope of Office or Employment at Time of Incident Out of Which Claim Arose (28 USCS § 2679(d))*, 120 ALR Fed 95.

50 28 U.S.C. § 2679(d)(1).

51 *Id.*

52 § 2679(d)(2). As noted on page 3 of this report, suits under the FTCA may be heard only in federal district court.

53 § 2679(d)(3).

54 *Id.*

55 *Id.*

56 A hypothetical issue of federal jurisdiction arose in the case, on which there was no majority opinion. If a suit against a federal employee is brought in state court and the Attorney General certifies that the employee was acting within the scope of his employment, the resulting FTCA case must be removed to federal court. Then, if the federal court rejects the certification and the employee is again made the defendant, what is the basis for federal jurisdiction? If the plaintiff and the employee are of diverse citizenship, then there is no problem, but, if they are not, then there arguably is no basis for federal jurisdiction. However, the plurality opinion found that the fact that, in this hypothetical case, "there was a nonfrivolous federal question [whether the employee was acting within the scope of his federal employment], certified by the local U.S. Attorney, when the case was removed to federal court," is an adequate basis to find that the case "arises under" federal law (emphasis in original). *Id.* at 435. All this was dictum, as there was diversity jurisdiction in the case before the Court.

57 "The Supreme Court uses the term 'constitutional tort' for any constitutional violation for which a court may award damages." K. Davis, 5 Administrative *Law Treatise* § 27:1 (2d ed. 1984).

58 In *Davis v. Passman*, 442 U.S. 228 (1979), the Court held that a Member of Congress could be found liable for damages for violating the Due Process Clause of the Fifth Amendment by firing a member of his staff because of her sex. In its opinion the Court indicated that all "justiciable constitutional rights are to be enforced through the courts." *Id.* at 242.

59 The statute of limitations for *Bivens* actions has not been addressed by the Supreme Court, but lower courts have held "that *Bivens* actions are governed

by the same state personal injury limitations period applicable to [42 U.S.C.] section 1983 actions... ." Cook and Sobieski, 2 *Civil Rights Actions*, ¶ 4.01 [B] (2006).

[60] In *Bush v. Lucas*, 462 U.S. 367, 368 (1983), the Court declined "to authorize a new nonstatutory damages remedy for federal employees whose First Amendment rights are violated by their superiors." The Court's reason was that "such claims arise out of an employment relationship that is governed by comprehensive procedural and substantive provisions giving meaningful remedies against the United States."

[61] The principle behind the *Feres* doctrine, however, should be distinguished from the doctrine itself, which applies only to suits against the United States. In *Cross v. Fiscus*, 830 F.2d 755, 756 (7th Cir. 1987), the court of appeals wrote: "The doctrine of *Stanley* and *Chappell* tracks *Feres* ... . But its source is different. *Feres* is a construction of a statute. *Stanley* and *Chappell* are constructions of the Constitution based on considerations similar to those that, the Court believes, influenced Congress when enacting the FTCA. If Congress amended the FTCA, the principles of *Stanley* and *Chappell* would be unaffected — though Congress could create a federal remedy against service personnel by passing a separate statute."

[62] In *Carlson v. Green*, the Court spoke of "special factors counselling hesitation" and the availability of an "alternative remedy which is explicitly declared to be a substitute" as distinct situations in which *Bivens* actions are unavailable. In *Schweiker v. Chilicky*, 487 U.S. 412, 423 (1988), the Court said that "the concept of 'special factors counselling hesitation ... ' has proved to include an appropriate judicial deference to indications ... that Congress has provided what it considers adequate remedial mechanisms." In *McCarthy v. Madigan*, 503 U.S. 140 (1992), the Court held that, where Congress had not required exhaustion of remedies, a prisoner could bring a *Bivens* action solely for money damages without resorting to an internal grievance procedure.

[63] In *Castaneda v. United States*, No. CV 07-07241 DDD (JCx) (C.D. Cal., March 11, 2008), the district court, after quoting the statement from *Carlson* that "Congress views the FTCA and *Bivens* as parallel, complementary causes of action," added that, although 42 U.S.C. § 233(a) — cited in note 46, *supra* — precludes a state tort action against Public Health Services employees, it does not preclude a *Bivens* action against them. This is because § 233(a) provides that "[t]he remedy against the United States provided by sections 1346(b) and 2672 of title 28 ... shall be exclusive of any other civil action"; section 1346(b)(1) provides, "*Subject to the provisions of chapter 171 of this title* [emphasis supplied by the court], the district courts ... shall have exclusive

jurisdiction of [tort claims against the United States]"; and chapter 171 (the FTCA) includes 28 U.S.C. § 2679(b)(2) — enacted by the Westfall Act, which is discussed beginning at page 18 of this report — which provides that federal employees' immunity from tort liability does not extend to suits for constitutional violations (i.e., to *Bivens* actions).

[64] Correctional Services Corporation v. Malesko, 534 U.S. 61, 69 (2001).

[65] Cornelia T.L. Pillard, *Taking Fiction Seriously: The Strange Results of Public Officials' Individual Liability Under* Bivens, 88 Georgetown L.J. 65 (1999). Department of Justice regulations at 28 C.F.R. § 50.15(a) provide: "Under the procedures set forth below, a federal employee ... may be provided representation in civil, criminal, and Congressional proceedings in which he is sued, subpoenaed, or charged in his individual capacity ... when the actions for which representation is requested reasonably appear to have been performed with the scope of the employee's employment and the Attorney General or his designee determines that providing representation would otherwise be in the interests of the United States."

[66] *Id*. at 66 (footnotes omitted).

[67] *Id.* at 80.

[68] In *Anderson v. Creighton*, 483 U.S. 635, 641 (1987), the Supreme Court applying the *Butz* qualified immunity standard, held that a federal law enforcement officer is not liable for participating in a search that violates the Fourth Amendment if "he could, as a matter of law, reasonably have believed that the search ... was lawful." In *Nixon v. Fitzgerald*, 457 U.S. 731, 750, 754 (1982), the Court held that "[t]he President's unique status under the Constitution" entitles him to absolute immunity from "private suits for damages based on [his] official acts." (He is not immune, however, for actions allegedly taken before his term began. *Clinton v. Jones*, 520 U.S. 681 (1997)). In *Harlow v. Fitzgerald*, 457 U.S. 800 (1982), the Court held that Presidential aides are entitled only to qualified immunity; specifically, they are immune unless their actions violate clearly established law. In *Mitchell v. Forsyth*, 472 U.S. 511 (1985), the Court held that the holding in *Harlow* applied even for acts performed by the Attorney General in the interest of national security. Additional discussion of the immunity of federal officials for constitutional torts may be found in Cook and Sobieski, 1 *Civil Rights Actions* ¶ 2.11 (2006).

[69] The Court noted "that a few areas, involving 'uniquely federal interests,' ... are so committed by the Constitution and laws of the United States to federal control that state law is pre-empted and replaced, where necessary, by federal law of a content prescribed (absent explicit statutory directive) by the courts

— so-called 'federal common law.'" *Id.* at 504. Justice Brennan, in his dissent in *Boyle*, objected that "[j]ust as '[t]here is no federal preemption *in vacuo*, without a constitutional text or a federal statute to assert it,' ... federal common law cannot supersede state law *in vacuo* out of no more than an idiosyncratic determination by five Justices that a particular area is 'uniquely federal.'" *Id.* at 517.

[70] The Supreme Court has held that in cases in which the United States is immune under *Feres*, a government contractor that is held liable may not recover indemnification from the United States because to allow indemnification would make the United States indirectly liable to the injured party. Stencel Aero Engineering Corp. v. United States, 431 U.S. 666 (1977). The Federal Employees' Compensation Act precludes federal civilian employees from suing under the FTCA for work-related injuries. 5 U.S.C. § 8116(c). The Supreme Court has held that, if a federal civilian employee recovers damages from a government contractor for a work-related injury, the government contractor may recover indemnification from the United States. The Court did not follow its reasoning in *Stencel* because, unlike in the military context of *Stencel*, "[i]t is clear that the Government has waived its sovereign immunity here." Lockheed Aircraft Corp. v. United States, 460 U.S. 190, 197 n.8 (1983).

[71] *See*, Sean Watts, Boyle v. United Technologies Corp. *and the Government Contractor Defense: An Analysis Based on the Current Circuit Split Regarding the Scope of the Defense*, 40 William and Mary Law Review 687 (1999).

In: Federal Torts Reform, Claims and Liability ISBN 978-1-60692-989-6
Editor: Ben V. Colligan

Chapter 3

MAKING PRIVATE ENTITIES AND INDIVIDUALS IMMUNE FROM TORT LIABILITY BY DECLARING THEM FEDERAL EMPLOYEES*

Henry Cohen

SUMMARY

The Federal Tort Claims Act (FTCA), 28 U.S.C. § 1346(b), 267 1-2680, makes the United States liable, in accordance with the law of the state where a tort occurs, for some of the torts of its employees committed within the scope of their employment. It also makes federal employees immune from all lawsuits arising under state law for torts committed within the scope of their employment. (The FTCA does not prevent a federal employee from being sued for violating the Constitution or a federal statute that authorizes suit against an individual.) Sometimes, Congress wishes to immunize a private organization, or its employees or volunteers, from tort liability. One way it may do so is to enact a statute declaring that the organization or its employees or volunteers shall be deemed federal employees for purposes of the FTCA. This chapter discusses the pros and cons of this type of statute, and then provides examples of more than 50 such statutes.

* This is an edited, excerpted and augmented edition of a Congressional Research Service publication, Order Code 97-579, dated July 11, 2008.

PROS AND CONS

The reason that Congress has sometimes declared private organizations or individuals federal employees for FTCA purposes is generally that it has concluded that potential liability, or the high cost of liability insurance, could discourage an organization, or its employees or volunteers, from doing the work it does. Thus, the basic argument in favor of these statutes is that, by immunizing potential defendants from tort liability, they encourage work that Congress deems to be in the public interest. In addition, because the United States has "deep pockets," these statutes can also benefit some plaintiffs. An injured party who prevails in an action against the United States is more likely to be compensated fully than one who prevails against a private party.

In general, however, these statutes probably leave injured parties worse off. First, they arguably remove an incentive for individuals protected by them to exercise due care in the performance of their duties. Second, they leave some injured parties with no remedy, because the FTCA makes the United States liable for only some of the torts of its employees. In general, the FTCA makes the United States liable for the torts of its employees to the extent that a private employer would be liable for the torts of *its* employees, under the law of the state where the tort occurred. However, the FTCA has exceptions under which the United States may not be held liable even though a private employer could be held liable under state law. These exceptions include suits by military personnel for injuries sustained incident to service, suits based on the performance of a discretionary function, intentional torts, claims arising out of combatant activities, claims arising in a foreign country, and others. In addition, the FTCA does not permit awards of punitive damages, and does not allow jury trials (and plaintiffs in tort cases tend to prefer jury trials).

The Supreme Court has held that the FTCA makes federal employees immune from suit under state law for torts committed within the scope of employment even when an FTCA exception precludes recovery against the United States. *United States v. Smith*, 499 U.S. 160 (1991). The same apparently would be the case with respect to organizations or individuals who are not federal employees but who are declared federal employees for FTCA purposes. Consequently, in considering whether to make a private organization or individual a federal employee for FTCA purposes, Congress may wish to balance the benefits of immunizing the organization or individual from liability against the likelihood of leaving potential plaintiffs without a remedy.

A way that Congress might protect both plaintiffs and defendants would be to allow the defendants to be sued but provide for the United States to take over the defense of the suit and to pay any damages for which the defendants are held liable. This way, plaintiffs would not be precluded by the exceptions in the FTCA from recovering against the United States. A partial precedent for this approach was the National Swine Flu Immunization Program, P.L. 94-380 (1976), which made an action against the United States under the FTCA the exclusive remedy for persons having claims in connection with the swine flu immunization program of the 1970s against vaccine manufacturers, but it removed or relaxed several of the FTCA exceptions that might have precluded recovery in some cases.

A statute may declare the employees of a private entity to be federal employees for purposes of the FTCA, but not declare the entity itself to be a federal employee for purposes of the FTCA. It may instead declare the entity to be a federal agency for purposes of the FTCA, or it may remain silent as to the status of the entity. If it declares the entity to be a federal agency for purposes of the FTCA, then the entity would be immune from tort liability, because, under the FTCA, only the United States may be sued. If it remains silent as to the status of the entity, then the entity presumably could be sued in addition to the United States (and would not have the benefit of the exceptions, such as the discretionary function exception, that protect the United States from liability). Perhaps, however, the entity could argue that, since its employee is a federal employee for purposes of the FTCA, its employee should not be deemed its employee for purposes of state tort law. If an entity's employees are not deemed its employees for purposes of state tort law, then the entity would not be responsible for its employees' torts. In deciding this question, a court would of course consider the language and legislative history of the particular statute involved.

LIST OF STATUTES

The following are examples of statutes that make private organizations or individuals federal employees for FTCA purposes, and thus immune from liability under state tort law:

(1) "[T]he Administrative Assistant, with the approval of the Chief Justice, may accept voluntary personal services to assist with public and visitor programs.... No person volunteering personal services under this subsection shall be considered an employee of the United States for any purpose other than for purposes of [the FTCA]." 28 U.S.C. § 677(c).

(2) The Commission on the Advancement of Women and Minorities in Science, Engineering, and Technology Development Act, 42 U.S.C. §

1885a note, § 5(i), provides: "Members of the Commission shall not be deemed to be employees of the Federal Government by reason of their work on the Commission except for purposes of — (1) the tort claims provisions of chapter 171 of title 28, United States Code."

(3) The Domestic Volunteer Service Act of 1973, 42 U.S.C. § 5055(f)(3), provides, with respect to volunteers in the ACTION Agency (including the Volunteers in Service to America (VISTA) program and the Older American Volunteer Programs): "Upon certification by the Attorney General that the defendant was acting in the scope of such person's volunteer assignment at the time of the incident out of which the suit arose, any such civil action or proceeding shall be ... deemed a tort action brought against the United States under the provisions of title 28. ... "

(4) The Federal Land Policy and Management Act of 1976, 43 U.S.C. § 1737(f), provides: "Volunteers shall not be deemed employees of the United States except for purposes of — (1) the tort claims provisions of title 28. ... "

(5) The Federally Supported Health Centers Assistance Act of 1992, 42 U.S.C. § 233(g), provides that such centers, and their officers, employees, and contractors, shall be deemed employees of the Public Health Service, and the FTCA shall be the exclusive remedy with respect to any medical malpractice they may commit.

(6) The Health Insurance Portability and Accountability Act of 1996, 42 U.S.C. § 233(*o*), extended the same protection as the Federally Supported Health Centers Assistance Act of 1992 to a "free clinic health professional" providing a "qualifying health service," which means an unpaid volunteer providing "any medical assistance required or authorized to be provided in the program under title XIX of the Social Security Act," commonly called "Medicaid."[11]

(7) The Fish and Wildlife Act of 1956, 16 U.S.C. § 742f(c)(4), provides that volunteers for, or in aid of programs conducted by the Secretary of the Interior through the Fish and Wildlife Service or the Secretary of Commerce through the National Oceanic and Atmospheric Administration shall be considered a federal employee "[f]or the purpose of the tort claim provisions of title 28."

---

[1] For additional information on this provision and the preceding one, see CRS Report RS20984, *Public Health Service Act Provisions Providing Immunity from Medical Malpractice Liability*, by Henry Cohen.

(8) The Glass Ceiling Act of 1991, 42 U.S.C. § 2000e note, § 203(h)(3). This statute, which was enacted by the Civil Rights Act of 1991, provides: "A member of the [Glass Ceiling] Commission, who is not otherwise an employee of the Federal Government, shall not be deemed to be an employee of the Federal Government except for purposes of — (A) the tort claims provisions of chapter 171 of title 28, United States Code."

(9) The Indian Health Care Improvement Act, 25 U.S.C. § 1680c(d), provides that non-Indian Health Service health care practitioners who provide services to individuals eligible for health services under the act may be regarded as employees of the Federal Government for purposes of the FTCA.

(10) The Indian Self-Determination and Education Assistance Act, 25 U.S.C. § 45 0f(d), provides that "an Indian tribe, a tribal organization or Indian contractor carrying out a contract, grant agreement, or cooperative agreement under this section or section 450h of this title is deemed to be part of the Public Health Service in the Department of Health and Human Services while carrying out any such contract or agreement and its employees (including those acting on behalf of the organization or contractor as provided in section 2671 of Title 28 [the FTCA] are deemed employees of the Service while acting within the scope of their employment in carrying out the contract or agreement. ... "

(11) The National Gambling Impact Study Commission Act, 18 U.S.C. § 1955 note, § 6(e), provides that, for purposes of the FTCA "the Commission is a 'Federal agency' and each of the members and personnel of the Commission is an 'employee of the Government.'"

(12) The National Guard Challenge Program of opportunities for civilian youth, 32 U.S.C. § 509(i)(1)(B), provides that a person receiving training under the National Guard Challenge Program shall be considered an employee of the United States for purposes of the FTCA.

(13) The National Guard Technicians Act of 1968, 32 U.S.C. § 709(d), provides that a technician employed under the act is "an employee of the United States." The act does not mention the FTCA, but apparently does make these individuals federal employees for FTCA purposes. See, *Proprietors Insurance Co. v. United States*, 688 F.2d 687 (9th Cir. 1982).

(14) The National Service Trust Act, 42 U.S .C. § 1265 1b(f), provides: "For purposes of the tort claims provisions of chapter 171 of title 28, United States Code, a member of the Board [of Directors of the Corporation for National and Community Service] shall be considered to be a Federal employee." It also provides that Corporation volunteers "shall not be

subject to the provisions of law relating to Federal employment ... except that — (i) for the purposes of the tort claims provisions of chapter 171 of Title 28, a volunteer under this division shall be considered to be a Federal employee." 42 U.S.C. § 12651 g(a)(B).

(15) The Peace Corps Act, 22 U.S.C. § 2504(h), provides: "Volunteers shall be deemed employees of the United States Government for the purposes of the Federal Tort Claims Act and any other Federal tort liability statute.. . . ."

(16) The Strom Thurmond National Defense Authorization Act for Fiscal Year 1999, 16 U.S.C. § 670c(d), provides: "In connection with the facilities and programs for public outdoor recreation at military installations ... , the Secretary of Defense may accept — (1) the voluntary services of individuals and organizations. ... A volunteer ... shall not be considered to be a Federal employee ... except that — (1) for the purposes of the tort claims provisions of chapter 171 of title 28, United States Code, the volunteer shall be considered to be a Federal employee."

(17) The Support for East European Democracy (SEED) Act of 1989, 22 U.S.C. § 5422(c)(2), provides that a volunteer providing technical assistance to Poland or Hungary through the Department of Labor shall be deemed an employee of the United States for purposes of "the tort claims provisions of Title 28. ... "

(18) The Take Pride in America Act, 16 U.S.C. § 4604(c)(2), provides that, for purposes of the FTCA, "a volunteer under this subsection shall be considered an employee of the government. ... "

(19) "[T]he United States Geological Survey may hereinafter contract directly with individuals or indirectly with institutions or nonprofit organizations ... for the temporary or intermittent services of science students or recent graduates, who shall be considered employees for purposes of [the FTCA]." 43 U.S.C. § 50d.

(20) The Volunteers in the National Forests Act of 1972, 16 U.S.C. § 558c(b), provides: "For the purpose of the tort claim provisions of Title 28, a volunteer under sections 558a to 558d of this title shall be considered a Federal employee."

(21) The Volunteers in the Parks Act of 1969, 16 U.S.C. § 18i(b), provides: "For the purpose of the tort claim provisions of title 28 of the United States Code, a volunteer under this Act shall be considered a Federal employee."

ADDITIONAL STATUTES

The following 32 additional statutory provisions listed in this paragraph also cause non-federal employees or entities to be treated as federal employees for purposes of liability: 5 U.S.C. § 3161(i)(4) (temporary organizations), 7 U.S.C. § 2279c(b)(8) (Department of Agriculture), 10 U.S.C. § 1588(d) (Armed Forces), 10 U.S.C. § 211 3(j)(4) (Uniformed Services University of the Health Sciences), 10 U.S .C. § 2360(b) (Secretary of Defense), 10 U.S.C. § 2904(c) (Strategic Environmental Research and Development Program Scientific Advisory Board), 14 U.S.C. § 93(t)(2) (Coast Guard), 15 U.S.C. §§ 4102(d), 4105(5) (Arctic Research Commission), 16 U.S.C. § 450ss-3(b)(5) (Oklahoma City National Memorial Trust), 16 U.S.C. § 565a-2 (Forest Service), 16 U.S.C. § 932(a)(3) (Great Lakes Fishery Commission), 16 U.S.C. § 952 (International Commission for the Scientific Investigation of Tuna, and Inter-American Tropical Tuna Commission), 16 U.S.C. § 971a(1) (International Commission for the Conservation of Atlantic Tunas), 16 U.S.C. § 1421e (Secretary of Commerce),[2] 16 U.S.C. § 1703(a)(3) (Youth Conservation Corps), 16 U.S.C. § 3602(c) (North Atlantic Salmon Conservation Organization), 16 U.S.C. § 5608(c) (Northwest Atlantic Fisheries Organization), 20 U.S.C. § 76*l*(e)(2) (Trustees for the John F. Kennedy Center for the Performing Arts), 20 U.S.C. § 4420(b) (Institute of American Indian and Alaska Native Culture and Arts Development), 22 U.S.C. § 2124c(i)(3) (Rural Tourism Development Foundation), 22 U.S.C. § 3508(d) (Institute for Scientific and Technological Cooperation), 24 U.S.C. § 421(b) (Armed Forces Retirement Board), 24 U.S.C. § 422(d) (Retirement Home Board), 33 U.S.C. § 569c (Army Corps of Engineers), 36 U.S.C. § 2113(f)(2) (American Battle Monuments Commission), 42 U.S.C. § 233(p) (persons who manufacture, distribute, or administer smallpox countermeasures, or who transmit vaccinia after receiving a smallpox countermeasure),[3] 42 U.S.C. § 7 142(b) (National Atomic Museum), 42 U.S.C. § 7142c(b)(2) (American Museum of Science and Energy), 42 U.S.C. § 12620(c) (Civilian Community Corps), 42 U.S.C. § 12655n(b)(3) (American Conservation and Youth Service Corps), 49 U.S.C. § 106(*l*)(5)(C) (Federal Aviation Administration), 49 U.S.C. § 20107(b) (Secretary of Transportation).

---

[2] This provision protects persons who, pursuant to the Marine Mammal Protection Act, "respond to a stranding," but they are not immune from liability for actions "that are grossly negligent or that constitute willful misconduct."

[3] The immunity for persons who manufacture, distribute, or administer smallpox countermeasures was provided by section 304 of P.L. 107-296 (2002); the immunity for persons who transmit vaccinia was provided by section 3 of P.L. 108-20 (2003).

The most recent statute that provides that non-federal employees shall be deemed federal employees under the FTCA is the Project BioShield Act of 2004, P.L. 108-276, which enacted § 319F-1 of the Public Service Health Act. Section 319F-1(d)(2) (42 U.S.C. § 247d-6a(d)(2)) provides that a person carrying out a personal service contract under the statute, "and an officer, employee, or governing board member of such person shall, subject to a determination by the Secretary, be deemed to be an employee of the Department of Health and Human Services for purposes of [the FTCA]." Section 319F- 1(d)(2), however, contains exceptions to the immunity from liability that the FTCA otherwise grants to federal employees: "Should payment be made by the United States to any claimant... , the United States shall have ... the right to recover against [the person deemed a federal employee] for that portion of the damages so awarded or paid, as well as interest and any costs of litigation, resulting from the failure ... to carry out any obligation or responsibility ... under a contract with the United States or from any grossly negligent or reckless conduct or intentional or willful misconduct. ..."

INDEX

D

E

R

S

T